Gavin

from
the Editor.

UNPUBLISHED POEMS
by Sir Thomas Wyatt and his circle

ENGLISH REPRINTS SERIES
No. 18

General Editor
KENNETH MUIR

ENGLISH REPRINTS SERIES

SIR THOMAS WYATT
and his circle

UNPUBLISHED POEMS

Edited from the Blage Manuscript by
Kenneth Muir
*King Alfred Professor of English Literature
in the University of Liverpool*

LIVERPOOL UNIVERSITY PRESS
1961

Published by
LIVERPOOL UNIVERSITY PRESS
123 Grove Street · Liverpool 7

© Copyright 1961
LIVERPOOL UNIVERSITY PRESS

First Published 1961

PRINTED BY EATON PRESS, LIVERPOOL 7

PREFACE

Acknowledgements are due to the Board of Trinity College, Dublin, for allowing me to edit the poems in this book. I have received generous help from a large number of scholars, including Mr. H. A. Mason, Mr. William O'Sullivan, Dr. John Steevens, Dr. G. K. Hunter, Mr. R. T. Davies, Mr. G. B. Townend, Dr. A. R. Myers, Professor A. E. Sloman, Dr. Dorothea Oschinsky, Mr. K. Povey, Mr. D. F. Cook, Mr. A. N. Ricketts and Mr. Herbert C. Schulz. I have also to thank the editors of *The Times Literary Supplement*, *The London Magazine*, *Essays in Criticism*, *A Review of English Literature* and *Notes and Queries* for permission to use material which first appeared in their pages.

Liverpool, Easter, 1960.   KENNETH MUIR

CONTENTS

INTRODUCTION

I

The poems printed in this volume are to be found in a manuscript (D.2.7) now in the library of Trinity College, Dublin. This is now bound in three volumes. All the contents came to the college with Archbishop Ussher's library in 1666. Some of the first volume, however, was bound up with the contents of MS. E.2.27 until 1742, and some of it was bound up with the contents of MS. E.2.12 (minus the first item in that MS) until the same date. The second and third volumes, with which we are now concerned, were a single separate volume until 1742, when this was bound up with the contents of the present first volume.[1] The poems in the second and third volumes are mostly arranged in approximately alphabetical order; but as they are copied in a number of different hands it seems reasonable to assume that loose sheets of different dates (c. 1532—1551) were arranged in that way. There is a fragmentary index (letters A and D only) of first lines at the beginning of the second volume in the same handwriting as that of the first twenty-two poems printed here; but some of the poems listed in the index are missing,[2] and space has been left for the first lines of other poems which might be added later.

---

[1] For these facts I am indebted to Mr. William O'Sullivan, the Assistant in charge of MSS.

[2] Seven poems are missing, including Wyatt's 'Absence abcentyng' (ed. Muir, No. 161).

The manuscript, or part of it at least, belonged to Sir George Blage (1512-1551). On f.61ʳ there is a fragmentary memorandum

thatt I george Blagge gentleman hatthe payd John Deyne . . . off Rochester the xxvith day of nouember in the xxviith yere of . . . for mysterys Whytte sumtyme one of the Abbey and monastery of Dartford.

This presumably refers to Elizabeth Whyte, who was a nun in the Dominican convent at Dartford. When the convent was dissolved in 1539, she received a pension of 100 shillings.[1]

Sir George Blage, the son of Sir Robert Blage, Baron of Exchequer, was born in 1512 and educated at Cambridge. He was a member of Parliament from 1545 to 1551, when he died. In 1546 he was condemned for heresy, but saved from the stake by the intervention of the King.[2] A long poem in the manuscript was written at the time when Blage was expecting martyrdom:[3]

> And I O Lord into thy handes do yield
> my faythefull soul apoynted now of the
> this lyfe to leue thoro fier in smythefild.

He survived into Edward VI's reign and gave evidence at Stephen Gardiner's trial. Another of his poems in the manuscript, in the same handwriting, but signed B.G., is entitled 'A remembrance of the dethe of the vertuous Lady Quiene Kateryne dowager Lat wyffe of the Lorde Thomas Seymor Vncle to the Kynge hys maiestie'. Katherine Parr died in 1548. There are two other Blage poems in the manuscript, one signed G.B., beginning:

---

[1] Cf. *Misc. Books of Court of Augmentations*, ccxxxiv, f.8 (quoted by C. F. R. Palmer, *Archaeological Journal*, XXXVI (1879), p. 267). I owe this reference to Dr. A. R. Myers.

[2] Foxe, *Acts and Monuments* (ed. 1846), V, p. 564.

[3] ff. 101-3.

Ryd of bondage free from Kaer seven yeres space and mor,
I fele no payne I knowe no greffe as i had doune befor.

The other, signed B.G., is apparently an elegy on Jane
Seymour. It begins:

Let the hethen whyche trust not in the Lorde
beweyl the ded and mourne apon the grave.

It compares the subject of the elegy to Hester,
Abigail, Lidia and Sara, and mentions that she found
favour with Henry VIII and that God sent her 'a
blessed byrthe'.[1]

Blage was in a good position to collect poems by
Wyatt and Surrey, for he was with Wyatt in Spain
between 1537 and 1539,[2] and he accompanied Surrey
to France in 1543, to take part in the siege of Landrecy.
He is mentioned by Leland as one of Wyatt's friends,
'*Ingenio Blagi delectabatur acuto*',[3] and Surrey dedicated
his version of Psalm LXIII to him, though they
quarrelled before Surrey's trial for High Treason.[4]
It is not surprising to find poems by Wyatt and Surrey
in Blage's collection.

II

The text of Wyatt has hitherto been based on two
major manuscripts (E, D), on three minor ones
(H, P, A), and on Tottel's *Songes and Sonnettes*.[5] Of

---

[1] The poems will be found on ff. 124, 152, 177. Another poem on f. 58
is partly illegible through damage to the MS. The only other poem by
Blage known to me is the savage epitaph on Lord Wriothesley who died
in 1550, which was printed by Nott from the Arundel MS. (ed. Surrey,
p. xcvii). Wriothesley was partly responsible for Blage's trial. It is
possible that other poems in the Dublin MS are also by Blage. In the
margin of 'At laste withdrawe your crueltye' (Wyatt No. 104) there is a
G which may stand for George. But it is not in the same handwriting as the
initials appended to Blage's poems in the MS.

[2] Cf. Nott, ed. Surrey, Ap. p. xxxviii; ed. Wyatt, pp. 296, 305, 345.

[3] Cf. Nott, ed. Wyatt, p. cv.

[4] Cf. J. A. Froude, *History* (1898), IV, pp. 217-8.

[5] E. Egerton 2711; D: Add. MS 17492; H: Harl. 78; P: Add. MS
36529; A: Arundel; T: Tottel.

these sources E is easily the most reliable, as it belonged
to the poet and was partly written by him.   The D
texts, as we can see by comparing its versions of poems
with the same poems in E, are less accurate.   Sometimes they may preserve earlier versions of poems
afterwards revised; and it is quite possible that some
of the poems printed as Wyatt's from D are not by
him at all.   The Dublin MS (hereafter referred to as
B) contains thirty-four of Wyatt's previously accepted
poems, and it is apparent from a comparison of the
texts that it is second only to E in reliability.   There
are about 250 variants in the 34 poems. The variants in
the E poems are of no great importance,[1] but the
variants in the remaining poems are nearly all superior.[2]
The three Tottel poems in B are particularly important,
as it is notorious that Tottel made unauthorized
changes.   The B texts of sixteen of Wyatt's poems are
printed in Appendix A.   It will be seen that several of
the poems are completely transformed, and that
nearly all are improved. It will be noticed, for example,
that in No. 104 B converts nonsense into sense; that
in No. 114 it supplies a missing line, in No. 156 a
missing word, and in No. 159 three missing stanzas;
and that the suspicious smoothness of the three Tottel
poems is absent from the B versions.

III

The Blage manuscript contains a known poem of
Surrey's, 'Such wayward wayes hathe loue', signed
H.S.   On the next page, in the same handwriting and
signed with the same distinctive H, is the poem 'Yf

---

[1] See Appendix B.

[2] Cf. K. Muir, *T.L.S.* (1960), p. 328.   The variants in No. 70 are also
important since half the poem is torn away in E.

Ryght be rakt and ouerron'. Although Tottel gave this among the poems of uncertain authorship, there is no reason to doubt that it is Surrey's too. A few pages earlier in the manuscript, in a different hand, there is the conclusion of a poem, signed with the same H, and followed by this quatrain:[1]

> He that spares to speak hathe hardly his entent
> He that speaks and speeds his speakyng is well spent
> He that speaks and speeds not his spekyng is but lost.
> and yet speakyng wythe owt spedyng is but a small cost.

IV

The Blage manuscript is a valuable anthology of poetry written between 1530 and 1550. Apart from previously published poems of Wyatt and Surrey, there are more than seventy other poems, the best of which can stand comparison with any others of the period, and they are generally superior to those of the anonymous contributors to *The Court of Venus* and *Songes and Sonnettes*. A few have already appeared in print. 'Fortune what ayleth the' was published in *The Court of Venus*; 'Some men would think of right to haue' was printed by Tottel, at first as Wyatt's, and then among the anonymous poems; 'Sustayne, abstayne, kep well in your mind' was printed by Ritchie from the Bannatyne MS; and two poems, not among the best, were included in Ault's *Elizabethan Lyrics*.[2]

---

[1] For the texts of the three poems, see K. Muir, *N.Q.* (1960), p. 368. Many of the poems in B are headed with the initial letter of the first line, for the purpose of arranging them in alphabetical order. But although the quatrain begins with H, the preceding poem begins with T, there is no other example in the MS of the second poem on a page being catalogued in this way—such poems were probably added after the index was made—and the H between the two poems on this page is quite different from those at the top of ff. 96, 97, 99. The H therefore belongs to the six-line fragment above it, not to the quatrain below it.

[2] XXXIX, XLV.

The present volume contains a selection of fifty poems from the manuscript, together with the two Ault choices and sixteen previously published Wyatt poems. Of the fifty, one of the weakest (XLVII), perhaps because of its corrupt text, is signed T.W. Another poem (XIV) is certainly Wyatt's too because the first stanza appears in D(No. 159) in the group of poems generally accepted as his. A third poem (XLIII) bears this inscription:

V. Innocentia
Veritas Viat Fides
Circumderunt me inimici mei

The last line is adapted from Psalm xvii.9.[1] The reference to the enemies that compass the poet round about, the protestation of innocency, truth and faith, words which surround 'Viat' as though to protect him, the Senecan refrain, *circa regna tonat*, the reference to the bloody days and to what the poet saw through a grate make it certain that Wyatt wrote the poem during, or soon after, his imprisonment in 1536 at the time of Anne Boleyn's fall. It is known that Wyatt watched the execution of the alleged paramours of the Queen from his cell in the Tower, that he half expected to share their fate, and that some of the victims were his friends.[2] The tone of the poem and of the Latin inscription is similar to that of other verses not included in the Egerton MS, though it has often been assumed that these were written after the fall of Cromwell:

---

[1] Ps. xvi in the Vulgate.
[2] Cf. *Crónica del Rey Enrico* (1874), p. 88. 'A todo esto que se hacia, estaba el buen Hihuet (Wyatt) mirando de una ventana de la Torre, y todo el pueblo pensó que tambien habian de sacarle á justiciar.'

Syghes ar my foode, drynke are my teares;
   Clynkinge of fetters suche musyche wolde crave;
Stynke and close ayer away my lyf wears:
   Innocencie is all the hope I have . . .
Mallice assaulted that rightiousnes should have . . .
Like as the byrde in the cage enclosed,
   The dore vnsparred and the hawke without,
Twixte deth and prison piteously oppressed,
   Whether for to chose standith in dowt:
   Certes! so do I . . .
Stond who so list vpon the Slipper toppe
   Of courtes estates, and lett me heare reioyce;
And vse me quyet without lett or stoppe,
   Vnknowen in courte, that hath suche brackishe ioyes.

These lines, like the poem under discussion, echo one of Seneca's choruses. Another poem (XXVII) expresses the feelings of one who was deeply shocked by the trial and execution of Lord Rochford, Henry Norris, William Brereton, Francis Weston and Mark Smeaton, who were accused of being Queen Anne's paramours. Smeaton is addressed by his Christian name, as he often was by others, and there is evidence that both he and Rochford were associated with Wyatt.[1]

There is no definite proof that Wyatt wrote this or any of the remaining poems in the Blage MS; but there is, after all, no certainty that he wrote many of the poems in the Devonshire MS; and as Blage was a close friend of Wyatt's and the compiler of D is unknown, the former was probably in a better position to collect Wyatt's poems that the latter. It is true that only two of the poems are definitely ascribed to him, but only one of the known Wyatt poems in the manuscript bears his initials; and the absence of these cannot be taken as an indication that he was not the author of other poems.

The poems in this edition are divided into three groups, according to the handwriting. The first group

[1] Cf. MS. Royal 20B. xxi.

(I—XXII) is written in a single careful hand; and in the same hand are seven of Wyatt's known poems.[1] On the evidence of style alone, several of the other poems in this group can confidently be ascribed to Wyatt; and, although some of them are uninspired, their weaknesses of rhythm and of repetitive vocabulary are characteristic of Wyatt's less successful poems. No. V reads like a translation of an Italian sonnet, and VII and XV read like some of Wyatt's original sonnets. The last poem in this group is one of the best, but a fragmentary version in four stanzas has been printed by Robbins in *Secular Lyrics of the Fourteenth and Fifteenth Centuries* from a Huntington MS (EL.1160). It is possible that Wyatt, or some other poet, was revising and expanding an earlier anonymous poem; but, as the handwriting of both fragmentary versions, which are written in the margin of an earlier manuscript, could well date from the period 1520-1540, it seems more probable that the Huntington fragment is a debased version of the poem given in B. As this contains two phrases and a complete line used elsewhere by Wyatt, it seems safe to conclude that he was the author of it.[2]

The next twenty-two poems (XXIII—XLIV) are in a different hand (or hands[3]) and this group also contains a number of Wyatt's known poems.[4] Another poem, as we have seen, is ascribed to Wyatt in the MS (XLIII); and I have suggested that XXVII is also his. Several of the other poems in this group are in Wyatt's style,[5] and though one would hesitate to ascribe all the poems in this group to him, many of

---

[1] Nos. 104, 150, 151, 167, 178 (printed in Appendix A); 20, 51, and one stanza of 67.

[2] See note to XXII.

[3] As some of the poems are carelessly written, it is difficult to be sure that they are all in the same hand.

[4] Nos. 5, 34, 66, 70, 72, 78, 87, 94, 105, 107, 156, 157.

[5] *e.g.* XXIII, XXIV, XXVI, XXVIII, XXXIII.

them are more like his work than that of any known
poet of the period.[1]

The third group consists of seven poems (XLV—
LI), of which three are in a single hand, in which there
is also a known Wyatt poem[2]. Of these three, one
(XLVII) is ascribed to Wyatt, one is manifestly his
(XLVIII), and the third is probably his (XLVI).

Of the fifty-one poems printed here, only three are
certainly Wyatt's; but one has only to read the anonymous poems in *The Court of Venus*, in *Songes and
Sonnettes*, or in any of the manuscript collections
printed by Flügel and others,[3] or compare the poems
of the period not by Wyatt and Surrey in any good
modern anthology with those of the Blage MS, to see
that either Blage's taste was finer, or his opportunities
greater, than those of the compilers of the other
MSS. There may have been men writing at the time
whose best poems were as good as Wyatt's, and who
wrote in his characteristic styles; but it is easier to
believe that Blage collected poems, which would
otherwise have been lost, by Wyatt himself.

In the notes will be found parallels between the
poems and those of Wyatt; and, since he was
notoriously repetitive, these parallels cannot be used
to show that the poems were written by an imitator.
Many of them are written in the stanza-forms of which
Wyatt was particularly fond, and the general tone is
identical with his. The poet bewails the unkindness of
his mistress and her 'false newfangledness';[4] he looks
back on the time when he was loved; he complains of

---

[1] The necessity for caution is underlined by the fact that one poem in this
handwriting was transferred by Tottel to the anonymous section of his
anthology, after being originally ascribed to Wyatt.

[2] No. 114.

[3] *Anglia*, XII, XXVI; *Archiv*, CIX, CVI; *Proc. Leeds Lit. and Phil. Soc.*
(1947).

[4] *e.g.* I; XXXVII.

being 'borne in hand'; he prays for patience; he longs
for death as a release from misery; he rejoices in being
at last freed from his slavery; and he laments the
cruelty of fortune.[1]   When he translates Italian
sonnets his rhythms are harsher than in his original
songs; he sometimes drops into alliterative metres; he
is fond of quibbling phrases ('Happe happith', 'fforce
perforce', 'cause causeles'); and he sometimes uses
very colloquial invective.[2] He begins a stanza with
the last words of the previous one, he varies his
refrains from stanza to stanza, and he begins a poem
with Latin words which appear also in the refrain.[3]
He quotes from Seneca; he translates or adapts
epigrams;[4] and he

breaks through the hypothetical world of fancy, with its artificial
emotions and studied address, and with fine imagination realizes
his experiences, and presents them in simple, fervent, and sincere
language.

This quotation was written by F. M. Padelford about
Wyatt;[5] and the description of the poet (or poets) of
the Blage manuscript given above could be applied,
by merely changing the references, to Wyatt himself.
Many of the poems, indeed, are worthy to stand
beside Wyatt's, whether he wrote them or not; and
there are at least seven which will, I believe, be
ranked with his masterpieces.

[1] XXXIII, XLVIII; VII, XI; XII; VII, VIII, XVIII; XXXVIII; III.
[2] V; XV, XVI; XIX, XXIV, XLII; XI.
[3] VI; XXX, XXXV, XXXVII; XLVIII.
[4] XLIII; XXIII, XLIV.
[5] *Early Sixteenth Century Lyrics*, p. xlv.

Poems

I

Alone musyng,
Remembryng
The woofull lyfe that I doo lede;
Then sore sythyng,
I lye crying   [5
As one for payne nere dede.

The vnkyndnes
Of my mystres
In great distres hath me brought;
Yet disdayneth she   [10
To take petye
And settith my hart right naught.

Whoo wold haue thought
She wold haue wrought
Such sorow vnto my hart,   [15
Seyng that I
Indeuered me
Frome her neuer to depart.

10 Yet]yt MS.

II

Absence, alas
Causeth me pas
Frome all solas
   To great grevans:
Yet though that I   [5
Absent must be,
I trust that she
   Hath remembraunce.

Where I her fynd
Lovyng and kynd,   [10
There my poore mynd
   Eased shalbe;
And for my parte
My loue and harte
Shall not reverte,   [15
   Though I shuld dye.

Beawty, pleasure,
Riches, treasure,
Or to endure
   In pryson stronge,   [20
Shall not me make
Her to forsake,
Though I shuld lak
   Her neuer soo long.

For ones trust I,   [25
Or that I dy,
For to aspye
   The happy owre—
At lyberty
With her to be,   [30
That pytys me
   In this dolowre.

III f.65

Alas, fortune, what alith the
Thus euermore to turment me?
Although that I onworthy be
    Thow wyl*not chaunge.*

Faynest when I wold obteyne, [5
Then thow hast me still in disdayne,
Wylt thow thus styll increase my *payne,*
    And *wylt not chaunge?*

Alas! doth this not the suffice?
What prouf yet canste thow more devyse [10
Then styll to turment me in this wise
    And yet not *chaunge?*

What shuld I more to thee now saye?
Sum hoppe in me doth rest alwaye,
Yet bound to thee I doo obey: [15
    When wylt thou *chaunge?*

Seyng there ys no remedy,
I wyll the suffer paciently,
Euer in trust at last, perdy,
    That thow wylt chaunge. [20

2 Thus]thys.   4, 7, 8, 12, 16 *italicised words have been torn off.*
7 Thus]this.

Unpublished Poems

IV

Alle ye that knowe of care and heuynes,
  My woofull fatte when ye haue hard,
  Then judge the truthe in this my great dis-
      tresse,
  Yf any woo may be therto compared;
  And marke my thought as I shall yt expresse,   [
  For cause hit self doth nother mar nor make,
  But euyn as the pacyent doth hit take.

I thyncke whoo soo doth behold my payne
  Sees the soule of sorow grounded in gryff,
  The rotte of woo portred in payne,   [1
  The cloude of care dispayred in Relyff,
  The lothed lyff thorow dartyd with dysdayne,
  Sorow ys I and I evyn the same,
  In that all men do call me by that name.

When I doo cast my carefull lok doun Right   [1
  Vpon the ground, as thoo that I wolld fall,
  Theryn me thynckes ys gravyn with my sight
  The pyctour of my sorowfull thoughtes all;
  Ye, and the wormes that appere agaynst the
      nyght,
  As me semes, they thynck that deth doth
      mych yll   [20
  To leve me thus to lyve agaynst my wyll.

Where I do vse to lye Right secretly,
  Apon a banck ouer a Ryuer clere,
  Soo ofte I there be wayle my desteyne
  That the water disdayneth hit to here,   [25
  And at my wepying takes great envy,
  Lest the teres that ffrome my nyes do rayne
  Shuld cause the fysshe theryn to morne and
      playne.

Alone when I doo walke the woodes wandryng,
　Vttryng my care with paynefull sighes and
　　　grevans,　　　　　　　　　　　　　　　[30
　The birdes, which on the bowes syt syngyng,
　To here my cry then ses they all attons,
　Hauyng great grudge at me and my wellyng,
　By cause yt was so grevous shyrle and lowde,
　That hit stonnyd theire song thorow all the
　　　woode.

6 cause]disease.　　　10 rotte]root.　　　10 portred]portrayed.
14 In]ine MS.　　　　20 they]the MS.　　　32 attons]at once.

V

Agaynste the Rock I clyme both hy and hard,
  When at the foote the forde doth bray so lowde
  That saue the hart so faythfully had vowyed,
  Seith frome the foote in medeway I was forward,
  No hart soo hardy nor corryge that cowld
  Aventure to clyme Soo hy a Shrowd:
  Hoppe byddes me hoppe of payne the right
      reward.
  Now past the vale of Daunger and Dispyt,
  Mounted the Rock of Loue and perfit Joye;
  Bayned in the forde Dispere to washe awaye,   [1
  Hoppyng hereafter frome Darke to fynd the
      Light,
  Brought to the hyiste, am of the Deptyst agast,
  For Dred to falle, my hand now hold the fast.

12 Deptyst]deepest.

VI

Alas! my Dere, the word thow spakest
  Hath smotte the Stroke within my brest
  Of Cruell Deth, sens thow forsackyst
  Me and my faithfull ment behest.
  Too long I shewed that word to here,   [5
  That doth renew my great onrest
    And mornyng *Chere*.

And mornyng Chere, which by dispayre
  For wante of hoppe ys myche increst,
  So that now past both hoppe and fere,   [10
  Of my judgement I know the best
  Ys Lyf a while in paynefull woo;
  And how soon Deth wyll pers my brest,
    I doo not *know*.

I do not know when, nor how sone,   [15
  The stroke thow smast within my hart
  Wyll blede me to a dedely sowne,
  But well I know, tho thow revert,
  Till yt do blede and I stark dede,
  I shall renew with dayly smart   [20
    This Lyffe I Lede.

This Lyffe I Lede and Lyve to Long,
  Agayn my wyll in ters to melt,
  Sens none ther ys may ryght my wrong;
  But I must fele that I haue felt   [25
  The Stroke of Deth, and cannot Dy,
  Gaylyd within the strongest belt
    Of Crueltie.

Of Crueltie and cruell Deth,
    Forst to abyde Extremytie,   [3
    And yet do lyve, thoo I want breth,
    To show further how cruelly
    My hoope ys turned to murnyng chere,
    And ye the cause thereof onely,
        Alas, my dere.

2 smotte] *orig.* stroke.   7 *Chere*] *word is torn off.*   13 soon] *orig.* shuld.
14 *know*] *torn off.*   16 smast] ?struck.   19 do] *orig.* doth.
31 yet] yt MS.   31 do] *orig.* doth.

VII

Be belstred wordes I am borne in hand,
    As whoo saith, byddyn I shuld obbey.
    Ye may thret twys, er ons ye maye
    Prevayle by poure to vnderband,
    That I shuld yeld and nat withstand.   [5
    Youre wordes doo well, your wittes bewraye
    Wenyng to bere so great a Swaye,
    To wene my will when ye commaunde.
    The ffre ye fforse by ffere,
    To seke obedyens of the thrall.   [10
    Youre thretenyng wordes of poer but small
    Ys wasted wynd to vse them here;
    For lyke aquytaunce of lyke scathe
    Ys my noo force of your no faith.

There is a later copy, in a different hand, on the same page.
  1 Be]By.   1 belstred]bolsterd *later copy*.
  4 vnderband] conspire?   11 poer]power.

VIII

Beyng as noone ys I doo complayne
  Of my myshapp, turment, and my woo,
  Wysshyng for Dethe with all my myght and
      mayne,
  For Lyffe ys to me as my Chief Deadly foo.
  Alas, alas, of Comford I haue noo moo;
  Left but onely to syng this Dulphull song:
  Paciens, parforce content thy self with wrong.

Euer I hoppe sum faver to obteyne,
  Trustyng that she wyll recompence at Last,
  As reason were, my passyng deadly payne;   [
  And styll I percevered, and they incresse soo fast,
  That hoppe me Left, and I, as all agaste,
  Had noo comford, but Lernd to syng this song:
  Paciens, parforce content thy self with wrong.

I Burne and boyle without redress;   [
  I syegh, I wepe, and all in vayne.
  Now Hotte, now Cold, whoo can expresse
  The thowsaund parte of my great payne?
  But yf I myte her faver Atteigne,
  Then wold I trust to chaunge this song,   [2
  With pety for paciens, and consciens for wrong.

11 they]the MS.

IX

Complaynyng, alas, without redres,
   This wofully do I my Lyfe Lede,
   My harte Lamentyng in heuynes,
   Through whose mekenes I am nere dede.

This I induer alwayes in payne,   [5
   Dewoyd of pyty as in this Case,
   Yet my pore Harte cannot refrayne;
   Wherfore, Alas, I Dy, Alas!

Soo vnkynd, alas, saw I never noone,
   So hard harted, so mych without pyty   [10
   As she to whome I make my mone;
   Wherefore, alas, I Dy, I Dy.

Where I Love best, I am refused;
   Where I am Louyd, I doo not passe;
   Where I wold faynest, I am dysdayned;   [15
   Wherefore I Dy, alas, alas!

Comforthles, complaynyng, thus I remayne;
   Merceles, remaynyng without remedy;
   Cruelnes incressyng through fals dysdayne,
   Pytyles remaynyng, alas, I Dy, I Dy.   [20

But from hensforth I hold it best
   Them for to loue that loueth me;
   And then my hart shall haue sum rest,
   Where now for payne I Dy, I Dy.

4 mekenes]unkennes (? unkindnes) *later correction.*

X

"Comeforthe at hand, pluck vp thy harte!
  Lok Lowe! se where hit doth stand!
  Synes the redresse of all thy smart
  Douth Ley soo good a hand,
    Pluck vp thy hart.

Pluck vp thy harte! Why Drowpest thow soo?"
  So Sayde I to my thought;
  And frome the Hile I loked Loo
  And with my nye I sought
    Comforth at hand.

Comeforth at hand my nye hath found;
  My thought, therfore be glade;
  Yf she be there may hele thy wounde,
  Why shuldyst thou then be sad?
    Pluck vp thy hart.

Pluck vp thy hart! A mornyng man
  Doth gett noo good by woo.
  Be glad alway, for whoo soo can
  Shall fynd, wher soo He goo,
    Comeforth at hand.

Comeforth at hand! goo seecke and fynd!
  Loke yf there be redresse:
  Yf not, abyde a better wynd,
  In hope of sum reles,
    Pluck vp thy hart.

---

1 &c. Comeforthe]Comfort.
4 a]at.
18 Be]By MS.
6 Why]Whey MS.
24 In]In soo MS.
1 thy]they MS.
7 to]*om*. MS.

XI

Do way, do way, ye lytyll wyly prat!
  Youre slyly slynkyng cannot you excuse,
  Nor wordes Dysymmblyd cannot hid that
  That wyll pere owt, yf oftyn ye yt vse.
  Yf ye thynke other, youre self ye do abuse,   [5
  For hartly Loue unspyd Long to Last,
  Yf ye asay, youre wyttes sore ye waste.

Yff yt be possible, that frome a fyer gret
  The blak Smoke shall not yssu owt,
  Or a fore a Cryppyll to halt and countefet   [10
  And be not spyd, then quycly goo aboute
  Vs to begyle; for truly without dowte
  We know the craft, the Lokys and the prys.
  Wherfore trust me yt ys hard to blere our yes.

Yff that we to you of this do speke,   [15
  For good wyll to make ye leue your folly,
  Then wyll ye not stynt till ye be wreke;
  And redy to swere and styll wyll deny
  That that ys trew, yet wyll ye neuer apply
  To youre own fawtes, but alwayes ye excuse.   [20
  Leve, fy for shame! ye make men to thynk and
      muse.

Ye thynck to cloke that cloked cannot be,
  And thincke to hide that open ys in sight.
  Alas! my thynckith yt ys a great pety
  Your self to bryng in suche a plyght,   [25
  That shuld vs cause to thynck ye light.
  Leue of, therfore: in faith ye ar to blame;
  Ye hurt your self and lesyth your good name.

---

1 prat]? prater.   3 Dysymmblyd]Dysmmled MS.
5 self]felt MS.   6 hartly]hardly.   10 halt]half MS.
11 then]them MS.   14 yes]eyes.   17 till]tell MS.

XII

Desyre to Sorow doth me constrayne,
Dayly incressyng my Smart and payne;
I Se there ys no remedy playne,
  But paciens.

Dispayre doth put hym self in prese   [
To cause my sorows to encrese:
I trust at Last that yt wyll sesse
  By paciens.

Good hoope doth byd me be content,
And not my self thus to torment,   [1
Promassyng me my hole intent
  Through paciens.

I wyll not stryve agaynst the tyde,
For well I Se who doth abide;
That sufferans to hartes desyre ys gyde   [1
  By pacyens.

10 thus]this MS.

XIII

Defamed gyltynes by sylens vnkept,
   My name alle slaunderus, my faut detect,
   Gylty, I graunt that I haue don amys.
   Shall I neuer do soo agayne, forgyve me this.

Betrayed by trust and soo begyled,   [5
   By promas vnjust my name defyled;
   Wherfore I graunt that I haue done amys.
   Wyll I neuer do so agayne, forgyue me this.

Accept myne Excuse for this Offens,
   And spare not to refuse me your presens,   [10
   Onles ye perceyue ye do refrayne
   From doyng amys, wyle I lyue agayne.

1 gyltynes]gyltles *later correction.*

XIV

Dryven by Desire I Dyd this Dede,
   To Daunger my self without cause why:
   To trust the vntrue, not Lyke to sped,
   To speke and promas faithfully;
   But now the prouf Doth verefy
   That whoo soo trusteth ar he knoo
   Doth hurt hym self and pleas his foo.

Sens that my Language without eloquence
   Ys playne vnpaynted and not vnknowen,
   Dyspache myn answere with redy vtteraunce: [1
   The question is youres or elles my owne.
   To be vpholdyn and styll to fawne,
   I know non cause of such obedyence.
   To haue suche corne as sede was sowen,
   That ys the worst: therfore gyve centaunce.   [1

But yf youre wyll be in this case
   To vphold me Styll, what nedith that?
   Seith ye or nay, my question was:
   So long delay yt nedith not.
   Yf I haue ye, than haue I that   [2o
   That I haue sought to bryng to pas;
   Yf I haue nay, yet reke I nat:
   Where aught ys got, ther ys no lose.

The ye desyred, the nay not;
   No gref so gret, nor desire so sore.   [25
   But that I may forbere to dote.
   Yf ye, for euer; yf nay, no more
   To trubbyll ye this: speke on therfore.
   Yf that ye wyll, say ye; yf not,
   We shalbe friends euyn as before,   [30
   And I myn own, that yours may not.

21 That . . . pas]*altered by a later hand.*
23 aught]*orig.* naught (*the line has been altered by a later hand but the other
    corrections are not improvements*).
28 on]in MS.   31 myn own]my nown MS.

XV

Dryuyn to Desyre, a drad also to Dare,
   Bitwene two stoles my tayle goith to the ground.
   Dred and desire the reson doth confound,
   The tonge put to sylence, the hart in hope and
      fere,
   Doth Dred that hit Dare and hyde that wold
      appere.   [5
   Desyrus and Dredfull, at Lybertye I goo bound,
   For presyng to proffer my thynckes I here the
      sonde.
   Back of thy Boldnes, thy corage passith care.
   This Daungerus Dought whether to obey,
   My Dred or my Desire soo sore douthe me
      troubyll,   [10
   That cause causith for Dred of my Dekey.
   In thowght al wone, in dedes to shoo me Dobyll,
   Ferefull and faithfull, yet take me as I am,
   Though Dowbell in Dedes, a inward perfit man.

1 Dryuyn]*orig.* Dryuyng.   7 my]me.   12 thowght]*orig.* wordes.

XVI

Dobell, dyuerse, soleyn and straunge,
    But I haue sped and skappt vnspyd.
    Thancked be fortune of frendly chaunge,
    The Dede ys Don and I not Denyed.
    My traught mystakyn, and I vntryed,
    Yf Dobbell Drabbes were soo Defyed,
    As worthy ys there wandryng wyt.
    I wysse with reson doth not sit:
    To Do and vndo, and Scapp vnquyt,
    For youre noo faith, such faute were fyt.   [
    Forborne for fere, nay Loue ys hit
    Wherby ys bound the body soo.
    Thancked be fortune of euery chaunce,
    Of my myshappe I thanck my self.
    Payne or pleasure, woo or welth,   [
    Wounded by wordes, and Lackes avaunce.

3 chaunge]chaunce MS. (cf. 13)　　8 sit]set MS.　　13 be]by MS (cf. 3)

XVII

Had I wiste that now I wott,
   For to haue found that now I fynd,
   I wold haue Don that I Dyd not;
   But fayned faith dyd make me blynd,
   And by great othes fixed in my mynd,   [5
   His faith to be faithfull to trust,
   The Dede now proued, I fynd vnjust.

Hit ys not the thing that I pas on:
   Of his faith though I had assuraunce,
   Of that no more I wyll trust one   [10
   Then of a thyng that lyeth in balance.
   Truth laide aparte falsed ys; his mayntenaunce,
   Euer Dubbell, neuer wyll be true;
   Roted at the hart must nedes contynew.

XVIII

Horrybell of hew, hidyus to behold,
　　Carefull of countenaunce, his here all clustred,
　　With dead dropy blude that down his face
　　　　rowled,
　　Pale, paynefull, and petyvsly persyd,
　　His hart in sunder sorofully Shyvered,
　　My thought a man, thus marvelyusly murdred,
　　This night to me Came and carefully cryed.

O man mysfortunate, more then any Creytour,
　　That paynefully yet lyues more payne to per-
　　　　ceyue,
　　What hardenyd hath thy hart this harme to
　　　　suffer?　　　　　　　　　　　　　　　　[•
　　Thy Doughtfull hope hit doo the but disceyue.
　　No good nor grace to glade the shalt receyve,
　　By payne frome thy payne then payne procure,
　　Soo bitter hit were then endles Deth to endure.

"Folowe me", Seith he, "hold here my hand.　　[1
　　To longe ys Dethe in ters to proue.
　　The se shall Soner quenche the brand
　　Of the Desyre that hath the thus ondon;
　　Or soner send the to a deadly sowne.
　　Hold in thy hand the hafte herof this knyfe,　[2
　　And with the blade boldely bereyve thy lyffe."

"Cum of", quod he. "I cum", quod I.
　　Then therwith, as my thought,
　　My brest I persyd paynefully,
　　My hart right sowne I hit raught.　　　　　[2
　　But, lord! alas! hit was for naught:
　　For with that stroke I dyd awake.
　　My hart for sorrow yet fele I quake.

7, 18 thus]this MS.　　9 yet]yt MS.

XIX

Happe happith ofte vnloked for,
  As men may se before theire yes;
  For he that Dayly Doth labour
  And studith all he can Devyse
  To bryng his purpose to affect,   [5
  Yet by mishap most commenly
  From his entent he ys abiect;
  And happe doth happe clene contrary,
  So that the prouf Doth verefye,
  As I haue wryttyn here before,   [10
  That happ happes ofte vnloked for.

Some to myshapp when they ar borne,
  Ar prefate by there Destyne;
  To sume, tho all the world had sworn,
  Fortune wyl not be contrary: [15
  This happ doth happ at his own lust.
  Sum men to welth and sum to woo;
  Sum tyme the stronge he throyth yth Dust;
  Sum tyme the lame he maketh goo,
  And the Starke blynd to se alsoo;   [20
  Sume tyme the hole he maketh sore:
  All this happs ofte vnloked for.

Sum by good happ ar braught alofte,
  And sum by myshap ar throwen doun;
  And sum by hap ar set full softe,   [25
  That thynck neuer for to come downe.
  But I wyll rede them to take hede,
  Seith hap doth turne soo sodenly,

Lest he by chaunge do chaunce them lede
Into sum trade clene contrary,   [:
And bryng hym low that was full hy,
And set hym hard that set full softe:
Vnloked for all this happes ofte.

13 prefate]predestined.   18 yth]in the
27 to]*orig.* for to.   29 he]*orig.* hym.
33 vnloked]*orig.* and loked.   33 ofte]softe MS.

XX

The answere

Evyn when you lust ye may refrayne
 To payne youre self thus wilfully.
 Nother new nor old I doo retayne:
 Hit ys naught but your fantesy.

Youre proffered seruice ys nothing Swete, [5
 Yet wold you fayne yt properly.
 I doo not love but wher yt ys mete:
 I chaunge nothing my fantesy.

Youre meate and Drynke though hit be gon,
 Ye toke enouff when yt was by: [10
 Or ye may call for more a noon,
 When hit shall please your fantesy.

Hit was youre febyll founded love
 That fancy, founded fowlyshely,
 That made me love, lenger to prove [15
 Shuch fowlyshe fayned fantesy.

Yf that youre fancy, as you say,
 Doth cause you playne thus petiously,
 Esely to turne, perdy you may,
 When hit shall please your fantesy. [20

Youre chaine ys long, thow you be bound,
 For ye leppe far and Diversly;
 To small effect your wordes doth sound:
 They come but of your fantesy.

As ye Dyd knyt, soo Dyd I knyt, [25
 Evyn slack for slack right wisely:
 I Dought yt mych your new fangled wyt,
 Which proued ys by your fantesy.

Thus to come playne withouten gryffe,
  Therto ye lust your self Apply.   [
  The smartles nedith no relyff:
  I am not Rulyd by fantesy.

2 thus]this MS.   18, 29 thus]this MS.   21 chaine]*orig.* chaunge
24 They]the MS.

XXI

I am redy and euer wyll be
    To doo you seruice with honeste.
    Ther ys nothing that lackys in me
        But that I haue not.

My pore hart alwayes and my mynd   [5
    Fixed in youres you shall styll fynd;
    To Loue you best reson doth bynd,
        Although I haue not.

And for youre sake I wold be glad
    To haue myche more then I haue had,   [10
    The Lacke wherof doth make me sad,
        Because I haue not.

For I doo loue ye faithfully,
    And ye me agayne right secretly:
    Of let ther ys no cause why,   [15
        But that I haue not.

Yff I you ons of that myght suer,
    Oure loue shuld increse and induer;
    To study therfore hit ys my cure
        How I myght haue.   [20

Such ar cald fredes now a Dayes,
    Which do muse and study alwayes
    Bitwixt yong Lovers to put Dylayes
        By cause they haue not.

But this resisteth all my trust werely,   [25
    That ye agayne wyll love me stedfastly,
    And let thy word pas as yt hath don hardely,
        Till that we haue.

But for this tyme, swete hart, adew.
    Contynew faithfull, and I wylbe true;   [30
    And loue thee styll, what soeuer insew,
        Although I haue not.

25 werely]verily.

XXII

I muste go walke the woodes so wyld,
  And wander here and there
  In dred and Dedly fere;
  For wher I trust, I am begilyd,
    And all for your Loue, my dere.

[

I am banysshed from my blys
  By craft and fals pretens,
  Fawtles, without offens,
  And of return no certen ys,
    And all for your Loue, my dere.

[1

Banysshed am I, remedyles,
  To wildernes alone,
  Alone to sigh and mone,
  And of relefe all comfortles,
    And all for your Loue, my dere.

[1

My house shalbe the grene wood tre,
  A tuft of brakys my bede,
  And this my lyf I lede
  As on that from his Joy doth fly,
    And all for your Loue, my dere.

[20

The runnyng stremes shalbe my drynke,
  Akehornes shalbe my foode;
  Naught elles shall doo me good,
  But on your beawty for to thinke,
    And all for your Loue, my dere.

[25

And when the Dere draw to the grene
  Makys me thynke on a row,
  How I haue sene ye goo
  Above the fayrest, fayrest besene,
    And all for your Loue, my dere.

[30

But where I se in any cost
  To turkylles set and play,
  Rejoysyng all the day,
  Alas, I thinck this haue I lost,
    And all for your Loue, my dere.   [35

No Byrd, no bushe, no bowgh I se
  But bryngith to my mynd
  Sumthing wherby I fynd
  My hart far wandred, far fro me,
    And all for your Loue, my dere.   [40

The tune of byrdes when I doo here,
  My hart doth bled, alas,
  Remembryng how I was
  Wont for to here your wayes so clere,
    And all for your Loue, my dere.   [45

My thought doth please me for the while:
  While I se my Desire
  Naught elles I do requyer.
  So with my thought I me begyle.
    And all for your Loue, my dere.   [50

Yet I am further from my thought
  Then yerth from hevyn aboue;
  And yet for to remoue
  My payne, alas, avayleth naught,
    And all for your Loue, my dere.   [55

And where I ly secret, alone,
  I marke that face a none,
  That stayith my Lyff, as won
  That other comfort can get non,
    And all for your Loue, my dere.   [60

The Sumer Dayes that be so long,
  I walked and wandred wyde,
  Alone, without a gyde,
  Alwayes thynkyng how I haue wrong,
    And all for your loue, my dere.   [6

The wynter nyghtes that ar so cold,
  I ly amyd the
  Vnwrapt in pryckyng thornes,
  Remembryng my sorowes old,
    And all for your loue, my dere.   [7

A wofull man such desperat lyfe
  Becummyth best of all,
  But wo myght them befall
  That ar the causers of this stryfe,
    And all for your Loue, my dere.   [7

19 on]one.   27 row]roe.   32 To turkylles]two turtles.
46 me]om. MS.   58 won]one.   61 walked]walke MS.
67 the]followed by a blank in MS.

XXIII

Dydo am I, the fownder furst of Cartage,
   That as thou seyst my nowne deth do procuer
   To saue my fayth, and for no new loues rage
   To fley Iarbes, and kepe my promes suer.
   But se fortune, that wold in nother age
   Myne honest wyll in perfayte blisse assuer;
   For while I lyvyd, she made my day short;
   And now wyth lyes my shame she doth report.

6 perfayte]persayte MS.

XXIV

f.

Yf I myght hau at myne owne wyll
    Suche fflud of tearis wherwith to drowne,
    Or ffyer so hott as Ætna hyll
    With fervent ffyere that I myght burne,
    Then shulde I ende this carffull paygne
    That fforce perforce I do sustayne.

Or yf the syghis of woffull hart
    Could cause my selffe a sonder brake,
    Then by that means I shulde departe
    My mornynge dayes, and so to wreake   [
    My weryede lyfe and carffull payne
    That forys perforce I do sustayne.

Or yf my hand suche happe myght ffinde,
    With sword or knyfe to ese my woo,
    Then shulde I ease my paynffull mynd;   [
    But syns my hap cannote hap soo,
    I must Abyd this carffull payne
    That fforce perforce I do sustayne.

Or yf I myght haue at my wyshe
    The hevyn to ffall to short my lyfe,   [
    So by suche chaunce I coulde not myse
    But I shuld ende this carfull stryffe
    That dothe increase the woffull payne
    That ffors perforce I do sustayne.

Or yf the yerthe at my request   [
    Had powere to opyne, as in my wyll,
    I know ryght well my weryed breast
    Shuld ned no more to syghe his ffyll,
    For then shulde end this carffull payne
    That fforce perforce I do sustayne.   [

3 Ætna]Ethena MS.   10 morninge]morninges MS.

I knowe not where my heuy syghys to hyd,
   My sorrowffull hart ys so vexyd with paygne;
   I wander fforthe as one without a gyd,
   That sekythe to ffynd a thyng partyd in twaine,
   And sse fforthe ronne that skant can torne
      Agayne;   [5
   This tyme I passe and wast ffull petuslye,
   Ffor Dethe yt ys owte off thy syght to bee.

I skantlye know ffrome whome commys all my
      greff,
   But that I wast as one dothe in seknes,
   And cannot tell whiche way comes my mescheff;   [10
   Ffor All I tast to me ys betyrnes,
   And of my helthe I have no sykernes,
   Nor shall not have tyll that I do the see:
   Yt ys my Dethe out of thy syght to be.

I leve in yerthe as one that wold be dead,   [15
   And cannot dye, alas! the more my payne.
   Ffamyshed I am, and yet alwayes am ffed:
   Thys contrary all thyng dothe me constrayne
   To laugh, to morne, to walle, to joye, to playne,
   And shall do styll, ther ys no remedye,   [20
   Vntyll the tyme that in thy syght I be.

Ther nys syknes but helth yt dothe desyer,
   Nor povertye but Ryches lyke to haue,
   Nor shypp in storme but stering douthe Requyer
   Harber to fynd, so that they may her saue;   [25
   And I, Alas, nought in thys world do craue
   Saue that thow lyst on hym to haue mercye,
   Whose dethe yt ys out of thy syght to be.

1 heuy]*orig.* hartye.   19 walle]wawl, wail   22 nys]*orig.* helthe.
22 helth]helt MS.   23 lyke]*orig.* ffor.   24 Nor]*orig.* but
24 stering douthe]*orig.* that my deth.   25 fynd]*orig.* have.
25 they]*orig.* She.   27 Save that]*orig.* Saving.   28 Whose]*orig.* That.

XXVI

I have benne a lover
   Ffull long and many days,
   And oft tymes a prover
   Of the most paynffull wayes;
   But all that I have past
   Ar tryffylles to the last.

By prouffe I know the payne
   Of them that serue and serue,
   And nothing can attayne
   Of that whiche they deserue;
   But those payngys haue I past
   As tryffylles to this last.

I haue er this bene thralle
   And durst yt neuer shewe;
   But glad to suffer all,
   And so to clok my woo;
   Yet that pang haue I past
   As tryffelles to this last.

By lenthe of tyme or nowe
   I haue attayned grace;
   And or I west well howe
   A nothyr had my place;
   Yet that pang haue I past
   As tryffelles to this last.

My loue well ner ons wonne,
   And I ffull lyk to sped,
   Evyll tonges haue then begonne
   With lyes to let my mede;
   Yet that pang haue I past
   As tryfflles to thys last.

[1]

[1]

[2]

[2]

[3]

Somtyme I lovyd one
  That lakyd well my suete;
  But of my dedly mone
  Ffayr wordys was all the ffawte;
  Yet that pang haue I past
  As tryfflles to this last.   [35

My stedffast ffaythe and wyll
  With ffayr wordes haue I told;
  Yet hau I ffownd them styll
  In ther beleve to colde;   [40
  But that pang haue I past
  As tryfflles to thys last.

In love when I haue benne
  With them that loved me,
  Suche daunger haue I senne   [45
  That we wold not agree;
  Yet that pang haue I past
  As tryffelles to this last.

Abssence of tymes or this
  Hathe doblyd my deasease   [50
  In causyng me to mysse
  That thing that myght me please;
  Yet that pang haue I past
  As tryfflles to this last.

To promys love ffor love,   [55
  And mak to long delayes,
  Hath mad me ffor to prove
  Of love the paynffull wayes;
  Yet that pang haue I past
  As tryfflles to this last.   [60

Ffull many tormentes more
　　In lovyng I haue ffound,
　　Whiche oft hathe payned sore
　　My hart when yt was bound;
　　Yet all that haue I past   [6
　　As tryfflles to this last.

Nowe gesse all ye that lyst
　　And jug enow as ye please;
　　For oftymes haue ye myst
　　In Jugyng my dessease;   [7
　　Be nothyng then agast,
　　Tho ye mysiug these last.

6 tryffylles]tryffyll MS.   21 or]ere.   68 Jug]g Iug MS.

XXVII

In mornyng wyse syns daylye I increas,
　　Thus shuld I cloke the cause of all my greffe;
　　So pensyve mynd with tong to hold his pease,
　　My reasone sayethe ther can be no relyeffe:
　　Wherffor geve ere, I vmble you requyre,　　　　　[5
　　The affectes to know that thus dothe mak me
　　　　mone.
　　The cause ys great of all my dolffull chere,
　　Ffor those that were, and now be dead and
　　　　gonne.

What thoughe to Dethe Desert be now ther call,
　　As by ther ffautis yt dothe apere ryght playne,　　[10
　　Of fforce I must lament that suche a ffall
　　Shuld lyght on those so welthy dyd Raygne;
　　Thoughe some perchaunce wyll saye of crewell
　　　　hart,
　　A trators dethe why shuld we thus be mone?
　　But I, Alas, set this offence apart,　　　　　　　[15
　　Must nedis bewayle the dethe of some begonn.

As ffor them all I do not thus lament,
　　But as of Ryght my Reason dothe me bynd;
　　But as the most doth all ther dethes repent,
　　Evyn so do I by fforce of mornyng mynd.　　　　[20
　　Some say: "Rochefford, hadyst thou benne not
　　　　so prowde,
　　For thy gryt wytte eche man wold the be mone;
　　Syns as yt ys so, many crye alowde:
　　Yt ys great losse that thow art dead and gonne."

A! Norrys, Norres, my tearys begyne to Rune   [2
   To thynk what hap dyd the so led or gyd,
   Wherby thou hast bothe the and thyn vndone.
   That ys bewaylyd in court of euery syde;
   In place also wher thou hast neuer bene
   Both man and chyld doth petusly the mone.   [3c
   They say: "Aləs, thou art ffar ouer seene
   By there offences to be thus ded and gonne."

A! Weston, Weston, that pleasant was and yonge;
   In actyve thynges who myght with the com-
       payre?
   All wordis exsept that thou dydyst speake with
       tonge;   [35
   So well estemyd with eche wher thou dydyst
       fare.
   And we that now in court dothe led our lyffe
   Most part in mynd doth the lament and mone;
   But that thy ffaultis we daylye here so Ryffe,
   All we shuld weppe that thou art dead and gone.   [40

Brewton, ffarwell, as one that lest I knewe.
   Great was thy love with dyuers as I here;
   But common voyce dothe not so sore the Rewe,
   As other twayne that dothe beffore appere.
   But yet no dobt but thy ffrendes lament yee,   [45
   And other her ther petus crye and mone.
   So dothe eche hart ffor the lykwyse Relent,
   That thou gevyst cause thus to be ded and gonne.

A! Mark, what mone shuld I ffor the mak more
    Syns that thy dethe thou hast deseruyd best,   [50
    Save only that my ny ys fforsyd sore
    With petus playnt to mone the with the Rest?
    A tym thou haddyst aboue thy poore degre,
    The ffall wherof thy frendis may well bemone.
    A Rottyn twygge apon so hyghe a tree   [55
    Hathe slepyd thy hold and thou art dead and
        goonn.

And thus ffarwell eche one in hartye wyse!
    The Axe ys home, your hedys be in the stret;
    The trykklyngge tearys dothe ffall so from my
        yes,
    I skarse may wryt, my paper ys so wet.   [60
    But what can hepe when dethe hath playd his
        part,
    Thoughe naturs cours wyll thus lament and
        mone?
    Leve sobes therffor, and euery crestyn hart
    Pray ffor the sowlis of thos be dead and gone.

2 Thus]this MS.   5 vmble]humbly.   6 thus]this MS.
12 those]those who   17 thus]this MS.   32 thus]this MS.
35 exsept]accept.   46 her]hear.   51 my ny] mine eye.
61 hepe]help   63 crestyn]Christian.

XXVIII   f.1

Longer to troo ye
  What may hyt avayle me?
  For ryght well knoo ye
  Ye sware hyt vnto me
  Styll for to loue me   [
  Alone and no moo;
  But ye haue decevyd me:
  Who cold haue thowght soo?

Yowr fayth and yowr othe
  Fly abrode in the wynd;   [1
  I woold be ryght loth
  To stay that by kynde
  Cold never yet fynd
  In change to say whoo:
  Thys mene I by your mynd.   [1
  Who cold haue thowght soo?

Your gret assuerance
  Full oftyms dyd glade me;
  But the parformance
  Hath as well made me,   [2
  As reson bade me,
  To lett your loue goo.
  Wyth lyse ye haue lade me:
  Who cold haue thowght soo?

But trust well that I   [2
  Shall neuer mystrust ye;
  I care not a fley;
  Go loue wher hyt lust ye,
  For nedes change must ye
  In wele and in woo—   [30
  In that most I trust ye.
  Who cold haue thowght soo?

Farewell, vnstabyll,
   For here I forsake thee;
   Tru love ys not abyll
   Tru louer to make the.   [35
   Therfore betake the
   To them that do knoo
   The ways how to brake the,
   Where I cold not soo.

18 oftyms]oftmys MS.   30 wele]well MS.   37 betake]I betake MS.

XXIX   f.12

Mornyng my hart dothe sore opres,
 That ffors constraynethe me to complayne;
 Ffor wher as I shuld haue redres,
 Alas, I cannot be loyvd againe.

I serue, I sewe, all of one sorte;   [
 My trust, my trayvell ys all in vayne;
 As in dispere without comfforte:
 Alas, I cannot be lovyd agayne.

Perdye, yt ys but now of late,
 Not long ago ye knew my paygne;   [1
 Wyll your Rygore neuer abate?
 Alas, when shall I be louyd agayne?

It ys bothe dethe and dedlye smart,
 No sharp sorrow can now susstayne,
 Then ffor to love with ffaythffull harte,   [1
 Alas, and cannot be lovyd agayne.

See note to XLV. 1 Mornyng]Moaning 18752. 3 as]om. 18752
5 I sewe]and sue 18752. 6 My . . . all]Yet me thynketh all is 18752.
7 As in dispere]And so I leue 18752. 8 Alas, I cannot]Can not yet 18752.
16 agayne]gayne MS.

XXX

Madame, I you requyere
　No longer tyme detrack;
　Let truth in you aper,
　And geve me that I lak.

Ye wot as well as I　　　　　　　　[5
　That promys ye dyd mak,
　When tyme I cold aspye
　I shuld haue that I lak.

Bothe tyme and place ye haue
　My fervent paygnes to slak;　　　　[10
　Nothyng, Alas, I crave,
　But onlye that I lak.

Whyche thyng me thynk ys deue,
　Remembryng what ye spake;
　Ffor yf your wordes be trewe,　　　[15
　I must haue that I lake.

XXXI

The Aunswere

Your ffolyshe fayned hast
  Ffull small effecte shall tak;
  Your wordes in vayne ye wrast;
  Ye get not that ye lack.

I wot, as ye shall ffind,
  The promys I dyd mak
  No promys shall me bynd:
  Ye get not that ye lack.

Tho tyme and place I haue
  To slyd yf truthe wer slacke,
  Tho styll ye crye and crave,
  Ye get not that ye lacke.

[

Bycause ye thynck yt deue,
  I spek that that I spake;
  And this word shalbe trewe:
  Ye get not that ye lacke.

[

13 deue]deve MS.   16 not]no MS.

XXXII

O what vndeseruyd creweltye
    Hathe ffortune shewed vnto me!
    When all my welthe, joye and ffelycytie
    Ar tornyd to me most contrarye.

My joye ys woo, my pleasure payne,   [5
    My ease ys trayvell—what remedye?
    My myrthe ys mornyng, hoppe ys in vayne:
    Thus all thyng tornythe clen contrayrye.

The place of slepe that shuld my rest restore
    Ys vnto me an vnquyed enymye,   [10
    And most my woo reuiuythe euermore;
    Thus all thyng tornythe to me contraryre.

I borne ffor cold, I sterve ffor hete;
    That lust lykythe desyre dothe yt denye;
    I ffast ffrom joye, sorrow ys my meate;   [15
    Thus euery joy tornythe to me contrayrye.

The place of my reffuge ys my exylle;
    In desdaynes pryson desperat I leye,
    Therto abyd the tyme and wooffull whyle,
    Till my carffull lyfe may torne contrarye.   [20

2 shewed]shew^t MS.   10 vyquyed]unquiet.   20 Till]tell MS.

XXXIII

f.

Ons in your grace I knowe I was,
 Evyn as well as now ys he;
 Tho ffortune so hath tornyd my case,
 That I am doune, and he ffull hye,
  Yet ons I was.

Ons I was he that dyd you please
 So well that nothyng dyd I dobte;
 And tho that nowe ye thinke yt ease
 To take him in and throw me out,
  Yet ons I was.

Ons I was he in tym past
 That as your owne ye did Retayne;
 And tho ye haue me nowe out cast,
  Shoyng vntruthe in you to raygne,
   Yet ons I was.

Ons I was he that knyt the knot,
 The whyche ye swore not to vnknyt;
 And tho ye fayne yt now fforgot,
 In vsynge yowr newffanglyd wyt,
  Yet ons I was.

Ons I was he to whome ye sayd:
 "Welcomm, my joy, my hole delight!"
 And tho ye ar nowe well apayd
  Of me, your owne, to clame ye quyt,
   Yet ons I was.

Ons I was he to whome ye spake:
 "Haue here my hart, yt is thy owne!"
 And tho thes wordis ye now fforsake,
 Sayng therof my part ys none,
  Yet ons I was.

Ons I was he before Reherst,
   And nowe am he that nedes must dye;
   And tho I dye, yet at the lest,
   In your Remembrance let yt lye
      That ons I was.   [35

29 Saying]*orig.* syns.

XXXIV

O crewell hart, wher ys thy ffaythe?
    Wher ys becom thy stedffast vowe?
    Thy sobbyng syghys, with ffayntyng breathe,
    Thy bitter tearys, where ar theay now?

Thy carffull lokys, thy petus playnte,
    Thy woffull woordis, thy wontyd chere?
    Now may I see thou dydyst but paynt,
    And all thy craft does playn Appere.

For now thy syghes ar out of thought,
    Thyn othe thou dost no thyng regard,   [
    Thy tears hathe quenchet thy lov so hot,
    And spyt ffor love ys my Reward.

Yet love ffor love I had A whyle,
    Tho thyn were ffalse and myn were true;
    Thy ffayned tearys dyd me begyll,   [
    And causyd me trust the most vntrue.

To trust why dyd I condyssend,
    And yeld my selffe so ernystlye
    To her that dyd nothyng intend
    But thus to trappe me craftyllye?   [2

O ffalshed ffaythe, hast thou fforgot
    That ons of latte thou wart myn owne?
    But slaklye tyede may slepe the knot,
    No marvell then tho thou arte gonne.

Myn owne but late assuredlye,   [2
    With ffaythe and truthe so justlye bounde,
    And thus to chaung so sodenlye,
    Eche thyng vpone thy shame shall sownd.

Eche thyng shall sownd vppone thy shame;
   Syns that thy ffaythe ys not to trust,   [30
   What mor Reproche ys to thy name
   Then of thy word to prove vnjust?

And ffrom thy wordis yf thow wylt swerue,
   And swere thou dydst them neuer seye,
   Thy letters yet I do Reserue,   [35
   That shall declare the owre and daye.

The owre and day, the tyme and where
   That thou thy selffe dyddyst them indyte,
   Wherin thou showdyst what dred and ffeare
   Thou haddyst ons spyed thy byllys to wrytte.   [40

Thys proffe I thynk may well ssuffyse
   To prove yt tru that her I speake;
   No fforgyd taylis I wyll devyse,
   But with thy hand I shall my wreake.

When tyme and place therto I see,   [45
   No dobt ther ys but thou shalt know
   That thou dydst payn me wrongffully,
   Without offence to fforge my woo.

And thus ffarwell, most crewell hart;
   Ffarwell, thy falshyd ffayth also;   [50
   Ffarwell my syghes, ffarwell my smart;
   Ffarwell my love, and all my woo.

4 bitter]better MS.   24 arte gonne]*orig.* begonne   25 but]*orig.* ssaid.
28 Eche]*orig.* Eke.   29 Eche]Eke MS.   34 dydst]dyst MS
47 dydst]dyst MS.

XXXV   f. 1

Sche that shuld most, percevythe lest
 The vnffayned sufferance of my gret smart;
 Yt ys to her sport to haue me oprest;
 But theay of suche lyffe whiche be expert
 Say that I borne vnsertayne in my hart:
 But wher jug ye? no mor! ye know not.
 Ye ar to blame to saye I cam to late.

To lat? naye, to soon methynke Rather,
 Thus to be intretyd and haue seruyd ffaythffully.
 Lo! thus am I Rewardyd amonge the other.   [▶
 I thoughe vnnysyd whiche was to besye,
 Ffor ffere of to late I cam to hastylye;
 But thether I cam not, yet cam I ffor all that:
 But whether so euer I cam, I cam to late.

Who hathe mor cause to playn then I?
 Ther as I am jugyd to lat, I cam;
 And ther as I cam, I cam to hastylye.
 Thus may I playn as I that am
 Mysjugyd, mysintretyd more then any man.
 Now juge, let se of thes debate,   [▶
 Whether I cam to hastelye, or to late.

XXXVI

Spytt off the spytt whiche they in vayne
  Do styk to fforce my fantysye,
  I am proffest, ffor losse or gayne,
  To be thyn owne assuredlye.
  Who lyst therat by spytt to sporne: [5
  My ffancy ys to hard to torne.

Altho that some of bessye witt
  Do babyll styll, ye, ye, what tho?
  I haue no ffeare, nor wyll not flytt
  As dothe the water to and ffroo.   [10
  Spytt then ther spytt that lyst to sporne,
  My ffancye ys to hard to torne.

Who ys affrayd? ye, let hym fflee,
  Ffor I full well shall byd the bront
  May grece ther lyppis that lyst to lye   [15
  Of bessye brayns as ys ther wont;
  And yet agaynst the pryk thay sporne:
  My fancy ys to hard to torne.

Ffor I am set and wyll not swerve,
  Whom ffaythfull spetche removyth nought;   [20
  And well I may thy grace deserue;
  I think yt ys not derely bought;
  And yf thay bothe do spyt and sporne,
  My ffancy ys to hard to torne.

Who lyst therat to lyst or louere,   [25
  I am not he that ought dothe reche;
  Ther ys no payne that hathe the power
  Out of my brest this thought to seche;
  Then though theay spytt therat and sporne,
  My ffancy ys to hard to torne.   [30

1 they]y^t MS.   22 derely]derly MS.   29 though]thou MS.

XXXVII   f. 1

Syethe yt ys so that I am thus refusyd,
    And by no meanys I can yt Remedye,
    Me thynckes of Right I ought to be excusyd,
    Tho to my hart I set yt not to nye;
    But now I see, Alas, tho I shuld dye,
    Ffor want of truthe and ffaythffull stedfastnes
    Of hym that hathe my hart onlye,
    Yt wold not be but ffals nuffanglydnes.

I set my hart, I thought, not to withdrawe;
    The proffe therof ys knowen to well, Alas!   [·
    But now I se that neuer erst I sawe
    Wher I sought gold I fond but brytell glas.
    Now yt ys this ye know, somthyng yt was
    Not so promsyed, the truthe ys so dobtles.
    Who ys my fo, who brynges me in thys cace?   [·
    I can none blame but ffals newfanglydnes.

Yet Reasone wold that trewe love wer regardyd
    Without ffayninge, wher ment ffaythffully,
    And not with vnkyndnes ys to be rewardyd.
    But this yt ys, Alas, suche hap had I,   [2
    I can no more but I shall me aplye
    My woffull hart to bryng out of distres,
    And withdraw my mynd so ffull of ffollye,
    Sythe thus dothe Raygne this false newfang-
       lydnes.

6 want]what MS.   8 but]*om.*; for *later insertion.*
12 sought]thought MS.   18 wher]wher yt ys *later insertion.*
24 thus]this MS.

Sythe I my selffe dysplease the,
　My ffrend why shuld I blame
　That from the ffawte aduyse me
　That Kynkoryd my good name,
　And mad my mynd to morne   [5
　That laughyt my lov to skorne,
　And bownd my hart allwaye
　To thynk this payne a playe,
　That wold and neuer maye?

Too led my lyffe at lybertye,   [10
　I lyk yt wonders well,
　Ffor proffe hath tought his propertye
　That allway payne his hell;
　But sythe so well I wott
　Theys kyndes of cold and hott,   [15
　Suche ffancyes I fforsake,
　That dothe ther ffredome lake;
　My lyst no more to make.

Grodge one that ffell the greffe,
　I laughe that ffell the gayne   [20
　Of ffredome frome the lyffe
　Wherby wyld beastys be tayme.
　As ffast and wak a bedde,
　With hart and hevy hed,
　That haue a hongery hart: [25
　To mak my selffe well ffed,
　That may Redresse my smart.

Sythe I have sleped the knot
    That dothe my hart inchayne,
    I lyk the loky lotte   [3
    To well to knyt agayne.
    So newly com to welthe,
    Shall I deceayue my selffe?
    Nay, set thy hart at reast,
    Ffor welthe, my new ffownd gest   [3
    Shall harber in my neast.

To mak a wyllffull band
    Wher I may well Reffus,
    To be a byrde in hand
    And not my ffredome vse,   [4
    To syng and sorow not
    Yf wyllyngly I dott,
    To skypp in to the cayge,
    Yt were a wylffull Rage.

---

4 Kynkoryd]cankered.   10 Too]*orig.* tyll.   34 nay]*orig.* may.
35 new]ne MS.   40 not]*orig.* at.

XXXIX

f.167

Thou slepest ffast; and I with woffull hart
    Stand here alone, syghing, and cannot ffleye.
    Thou slepyst ffast, when crewell love his darte
    On me dothe cast, Alas! so paynefullye.
    Thou slepyst fast, and I all ffull of smart   [5
    To the my fo in vayn do call and crye.
    And yet methinkes, though that thou slepyst
      ffast,
    Thou dremyst styll whiche way my lyf to wast.

7 though that thou]thou y^t MS.

XL

Tho some do grodge to se me joye,
    Fforcynge ther spytte to slak my helthe,
    Ther false mystrust shall neuer noy
    So long as thou dost wyll my welthe;
    Ffor tho theay frowne, ffull well I knowe   [
    No power theaye haue to fforge my woo.
    Then grodge who lyst, I shall not sease
. To seke and sew ffor my Redres.

Whylest lyffe doth last and thou content,
    What shulde I dobt, what shuld I dred   [1
    Ther spyet that daylye dothe consent
    To make my joy ffrome me be led?
    What shulde I bowe to ffrend or ffoo.
    That wold me so thi syght fforgoo?
    What shuld I do, but passe full leght   [1
    The ffrayle mystrust of all ther spyet?

Yf cause were gevyne of any part
    To cause mystrust in them to spryng,
    Nought shuld yt greve me then to smart;
    But, I, Alas, know none suche thynge.   [20
    Then by myshappe and crewell lott,
    Thowe thaye wold so, forsake me not;
    Nor wyll me not my ffoos to please,
    To slake the sewte of all my ease.

Thyne owne and thyne for euermore   [25
    I am and must contynew styll.
    No woo nor paynes, no hurt nor sore
    Can cause me fflee frome this my wyll
    Thi owne to be, and not to start
    As long as lyfe ys in my hart.   [30
    Then graunt me this my lyfe to saue;
    As I desyrve, so let me haue.

25 Thyne]*orig.* youre.

XLI

Tho of the sort ther be that ffayne
   And cloke ther craft to serve ther turne,
   Shall I, Alas, that trewlye mene,
   Ffor ther offence thus gyltles burne;
   And yf I bye ther ffawt to dere,   [5
   That ther vntruthe thus hett my ffyere,
      Then haue I wronge.

Tho ffraylte fayle not to appere
   In them that wayle as well as I,
   And though the ffals by lycke desyere   [10
   Dothe swere hym selfe thyn owne to bee,
   Yf thou dost judge me one of theys
   That so can fayne suche commone ways,
      Then haue I wronge.

Tho chaunse hathe powere to chaunge thy love,   [15
   That all by chaunce ther wyll dothe gyd,
   Suche chaunce may not my hart remove,
   For I by chose my selfe haue tryed;
   And not by chaunce, wherfore I saye,
   Yf thou dost not my wylffare staye,   [20
      Then haue I wronge.

Thow stedffastnes in them do lacke,
   That do protest the contrayrye,
   And tho perfformans none theay make
   Of that theay promyse diuerslye,   [25
   Yet syns ther ffawtis ar none of myne,
   Yf thou Reffussyst me for thyne,
      Then haue I wronge.

5 bye]buy.   10 though]thou MS.   11 hym]them hym MS.
12 thou]tho MS.   13 ways]wavys MS.   15 chaunse]*orig.* chaunge.
18 chose]choice.   22 thow]though.

XLII

What wolde ye mor of me, your slav, Requyere
    Then ffor to aske and haue that ye desyre?
    Yet I Remaygne without recure.
    I insuere ther ys no ffaythffull harte
    That without cause causles that sufferth smart.   [

You haue the joy, and I haue all the payne;
    Yours the pleasore and I in woo Remaygne.
    Alas! and why do ye me blame
    Yt ys no gam, thus to destroye my hart,
    Nor without cause thus to cause yt smart.   [1

I haue assayed in all that euer I myght
    You ffor to please, ffor that was my delyght.
    All could not serue: ye lyst not see,
    But crewelly hathe vndone my pore hart,
    And without cause dothe cause yt suffer smart.   [1

Ye mak a play at all my woo and greffe,
    And yet Alas! Amonge all my myscheffe
    Nothyng at all that ye regard,
    Nor wyll Reward a ffaythfful menyng hart,
    But thus causles to cause yt suffer smart.   [20

If that ye lyst my paynffull dethe to see
    Ye ned no more but vse this creweltye;
    Ffor shorter dethe cannot be ffownd
    Then without grownd by force of crewell hart
    Causeles by cause to cause me suffer smart.   [25

A Deue! ffarwell! I ffell my joyes destresse.
    Ffled ys my welthe, my tormentis dothe encres.
    Thus haue I woone ffor all my hyere
    To brynne in ffyer sweltyng my woffull hart,
    That without cause causles thus suffreth smart.   30

9, 20 thus]this MS.

XLIII

Who lyst his welthe and eas Retayne,
   Hym selffe let hym vnknowne contayne;
   Presse not to ffast in at that gatte
   Wher the Retorne standes by desdayne:
   For sure, *circa Regna tonat*.   [5

The hye montaynis ar blastyd oft,
   When the lowe vaylye ys myld and soft;
   Ffortune with helthe stondis at debate;
   The ffall ys grevous ffrome Aloffte:
   And sure, *circa Regna tonat*.   [10

These blodye dayes haue brokyn my hart;
   My lust, my youth dyd then departe,
   And blynd desyre of astate;
   Who hastis to clyme sekes to reuerte:
   Of truthe, *circa Regna tonat*.   [15

The bell towre showed me suche syght
   That in my hed stekys day and nyght;
   Ther dyd I lerne out of a grate,
   Ffor all vauore, glory or myght,
   That yet *circa Regna tonat*.   [20

By proffe, I say, ther dyd I lerne,
   Wyt helpythe not deffence to yerne,
   Of innocence to pled or prate;
   Ber low, therffor, geve god the sterne,
   Ffor sure, *circa Regna tonat*.

19 vauore]favour.   21 ther]the MS.   22 yerne]earn.

XLIV

Venus, in sport to please therwith her dere,
    Dyd on the helm off myghty Mars the red.
    Hys spere she toke, hys targe she myght not
        stere;
    She lokt as tho her foys shuld all be ded,
    So wantonly she frownyth wyth her chere.   [
    Priapus can smyle and sayd; "Doway for dred,
    Do way, maddame, theys wepyns gret and grym.
    I, I for you am wepyn fytt and trym."

4 foys]foes.   6 can]gan.   6 for dred]fordled ?MS.

XLV

Alas! dere harte, what happe had I,
  Yf that I myght youre grace attayne!
  And sens I loue you faythfully,
  Why should ye not loue me agayne?

My Thynkes of right ye should me loue,   [5
  For well ye know I doo not fayne,
  Nor neuer shall ye other proue;
  Therfore, swete hart, loue me agayne.

I dare well say, yf that ye knew
  How long that I haue suffered payne,   [10
  Ye wold not chaunge me for no new,
  But euyn of ryght loue me agayne.

For as youre owne, ye may be sure,
  Ye haue my hart styll to remayne;
  Hyt lyeth in you me to recure: [15
  Therefore, swet hart, loue me agayne.

In hopp I lyve, and haue doone long,
  Trustyng yet styll for to optayne;
  And sure, me thynkes, I haue great wrong,
  Yf that I be not loved agayne.   [20

This poem, preceded by the first two stanzas of XXIX is also in Add. MS. 18752.
1 happe]hoppe MS.; hap 18752.   3 faythfully]faytfully MS.

XLVI   f.

Dysdayne not, madam, on hym to louke,
　　Whom sumtyme you haue louyd;
　　And, tho you forswar yt on a bouke,
　　Error yt may be prouyd:
　　Tho now your loue be gon and spent,
　　May happe you may yt soon repent.

Syns that hieraufter coums not yet,
　　Nor now ys so good as than,
　　Yet throw hym not doun, but let hym syt,
　　That so longe hathe been your man: [1
　　The tym may comm he may you ees,
　　Wyche now so soor dothe you dysplees.

Onys I was he that now I am not;
　　Your selff knos thys full well.
　　My mynd you kno wel enou by rot—   [1
　　You nyd no fashion to spell:
　　Feyr wourds to you I use,
　　Tho that you cruelly me refuse.

What tho nu broum suype very clyne,
　　Yet cast not the olde awey;   [2
　　That seruys not sumtym ys often syen
　　To serue well a nouther dey:
　　And store of housolde ys well had,
　　To kype the best and leue the bad.

---

1 to]too MS.   2 whom]wohem MS.   5 now]nou MS.
9 throw]thro MS.   12 now]nou MS.   10 longe]logne MS.
13 now]nou MS.   15 rot]rote.   16 fashion]fastn MS.

XLVII

Lyue thowe gladly, yff so thowe may:
  Pyne thou not in loukynge for me;
  Syns that dispayr hathe shut thy wey,
  Thoue to see me, or I to see the.

Make thoue a vertu of a constreynte;   [5
  Deme no faulte wer non ys wourthy;
  Myn ys to muche, what nedes thy playnt?
  God he knoythe who ys for me.

Cast apon the Lorde thy cuer,
  Prey ounto hym thy cause to urge;   [10
  Belyue, and he shall send recur:
  Vayne ys all trust of mans refuge.

3 thy]they MS.   8 God]Grd MS.   8 for me]me for me MS.
(Line 8 is partly illegible, with some deleted words. Possibly the copyist
began to write 'God he knoweth their hearts . . .').

XLVIII

Quondam was I in my Ladys gras,
  I thynk as well as nou be you;
  And when that you haue trad the tras,
  Then shal you kno my woordes be tru,
    That quondam was I.

Quondam was I. She seyd for euer:
  That euer lastyd but a short whyl;
  Promis mad not to dysseuer.
  I thoght she laughte—she dyd but smyl,
    Than quondam was I.

[ ]

Quondam was I: he that full oft lay
  In hyr armes wythe kissis many whon.
  Yt is enou that thys I may saey:
  Tho amonge the moo, nou I be gon,
    Yet quondam was I.

[ ]

Quondam was I: yet she wyl you tell
  That syns the ouer she was furst borne
  She neuer louyd non halffe so well
  As you. But what altho she had sworne,
    Suer quondam was I.

---

1 gras]grace.   9 thoght]thogt MS.   11 full]foul MS.
12 armes[harmes MS. 12 whon]a one.   14 amonge]anogne MS.
17 ouer]hour.

XLIX

Myght I as well within my songe belaye
   The thinge I wolde, as in my hart I maye,
   Repentens shulde drawe frome those eyes
   Salt tearis, with cryes, remorce, and grudge of
      harte,
   Causles by cause that I haue ssuffred smart.   [5

Or myght I ellis enclose my paynfull breast,
   That that myght be in syght, my great vnrest,
   Ther shulde ye see tormentes remayn,
   As hell of payne to move your crewell hart,
   Causles by cause that I haue suffred smart.''   [10

Ther ys in hell no such a feruent fyere
   As secret hete of inward hotte desyere,
   That wyll not let the flame appayre
   That I haue here within my wastyd hart,
   Causles by cause that I haue suffred smart.   [15

Yet you cause yt, and ye may cause my welthe;
   Ons cause yt, then retorne vnto my helthe;
   And of all mene releve that man
   That nothyng can but crye: ''Releve this hart,
   Causles by cause that I haue suffred smart.''   [20

Redres ye ought that harme that ye haue donne,
   Yt ys no game that ye nowe haue bygonne;
   But worthye blame ye shall remayne
   To do hym payne that knowthe not thought of
      hart,
   Causeles by cause that I haue suffred smart.   [25

8 tormentes remayn]*orig.* MS.; the tormentes give *later corr.*

L

My swet, alas, fforget me not,
 That am your owne ffull suer posseste;
 And ffor my part, as well ye woot,
 I cannot swarue ffrome my behest;
 Sens that my lyffe lyethe in your lott,
 At this my pore and just request,
  Fforget me not.

Ye wott how suer that I am tryed,
 My menyng clene devoyde of blott;
 Yours ys the proffe; ye haue me tryed, [•
 And in my swet ye ffound no spott;
 Of all my welthe and helthe is the gyd,
 That of my lyff doth knyt the knot,
  Fforget me not.

Ffor yours I am and wilbe styll, [1
 Although dalye ye se me not;
 Sek ffor to saue, that ye may spyll,
 Syns of my lyffe ye hold the shott;
 Then grant me this ffor my goodwyll,
 Whiche ys but Ryght, as god yt wot, [2•
  Fforget me not.

Consyder how I am your thrall,
 To serue you bothe in cold and hott;
 My ffawtes ffor thinking nought at all ,
 In prisone strong tho I shuld Rott; [2•
 Then in your earys let petye ffall,
 And leste I peryshe, in your lott
  Fforget me not.

---

23 hott]heat MS.   27 leste]lesse MS.

LI

Syns Loue ys founde wythe parfytnes
  And longe tyme growen within your hart,
  I moust therfor, of gentylnes,
  Regarde your paynes and greuous smart.
  My Loue from you shale no wyse part   [5
    In welthe ande woo, in care and Joye:
    Mon cuer aues pense de moy.

Thowghe falce mystrust doth banyshe our pre-
        sence,
  Wythe priue dysdayne that Loue woulde dis-
        seuer,
  Yet shal our hartes be tru in absence,   [10
  In faythfull Loue styll too perseuer.
  Chaunce as yt wyll, thowghe chawnce coume
      niuer.
    In welthe ande woo, in care and Joye:
    Mon cuer aues pense de moy.

Myne eyes be closyd, I may not see;   [15
  Myne eres be stopt, I may not here;
  Yet ys my hart at lyberte
  On you to thynke bothe far ande nere.
  No erthely creature shall change my cheyr.
    In welthe ande woo, in care and Joye: [20
    Mon cuer aues pense de moy.

I sey no more: in chaunce ys alle.
  Sumwhat I thynke, thowghe lytle I saye;
  But of one thynge be sure ye shalle
  To haue of me as mooche as may,   [25
  To be your coumfort nyt and dey.
    In welthe ande woo, in care and Joye:
    Mon cuer aues pense de moy.

5 aues] *avez.*

Notes

I.   Wyatt uses the same stanza form. Cf. ed. Muir Nos. 86, 123, 156. 18 neuer to depart] Cf. No. 13. 15.

II.   Wyatt uses this stanza. Cf. Nos. 51, 155.
15 revert] Cf. Nos. 53.15, 69.19. 20 pryson stronge] Cf. L.55.

III.   Cf. No. 150 and similar refrains in Nos. 58, 66, 72-4, 77 &c.
4 chaunge] one of Wyatt's favourite words. Cf. No. 5.13, 10.1, &c.
6 disdayne] another favourite. Cf. Nos. 1.7, 2.7, 5.22, &c.
7 payne] another favourite. Cf. Nos. 1.2, 2.1, 4.10, 5.19, &c.
17 remedy] another favourite. Cf. Nos. 43,28, 66.14, &c.

IV.   Cf. Nos. 5, 8, 22, 37, &c.
22-8 Cf. No. 22.8-14.

V.   Possibly a translation of an Italian sonnet, with a line missing from the octave.

VI.   Wyatt elsewhere uses the device of beginning a stanza with the last words of the previous one. Cf. Nos. 36, 121.

VII.   Cf. Wyatt's original sonnets, Nos. 16, 160.
1 borne in hand] Cf. Nos. 14.13, 152.23, 158.15.
12 wasted wynd] Cf. No. 48.1

VIII.   7 paciens, parforce] Cf. No. 39.1-3 Patience . . . of force; No. 40.13 Paciens, no force; No. 118.37; No. 162.1 Patiens, for I have wrong. 15 redres] one of Wyatt's favourite words. Cf. Nos. 2.12, 6.6, 15.3, 22.12, 39.12, 57.13, 65.27, 72.11, 74.9, 84.46, 89.11, &c.

IX.   1 redres] See previous note. 12 I Dy] Cf. No. 70.4. 18 remedy] Cf. note to III.17.

X.   3 redresse] See note to VIII.15. 3 smart] another of Wyatt's favourite words. Cf. Nos. 5.1, 8.16, 11.16, 20.5, 157.5, 10 for redresse . . . Of all my smarte.

XII.   2 incressyng my Smart] Cf. No. 89.5 encrease my smarte. 3-4 remedy . . . But paciens] Cf. No.

118.23-4 I se no Remedy But suffer pacyently;
No. 163.28 Wythe patiens for remedye. Cf. also
Nos. 39, 40, 47, 187. 13 I wyll not stryve agaynst
the tyde] Cf. No. 155.20.

XIII. 1 The corrector misunderstood. 3 Gylty, I graunt that
I haue don amys Cf. Nos. 125.6, 125.27.

XIV. 1-7 This stanza is also in D. Cf. No. 159. 30-1 yf not,
We shalbe frendes euyn as before] Cf. No. 34.10
If it be nay, frendes as before.

XV. 6 at Lybertye I goo bound] Cf. No. 21.11 Imprisoned in
libertes; No. 56.8 Twixt hope and drede locking my
libertie; No. 164.32 Wherein is bounde my liberte.

XVI. 3 Thancked be fortune] Cf. No. 37.8, No. 125.3. For
the rhythm of this poem cf. No. 160.

XVII. 4 fayned faith] Cf. Nos. 158.15, 163.22. 8 pas on] Cf.
No. 19.6.

XVIII. Wyatt occasionally uses such a mixture of alliterative
and rhymed verse. Cf. Nos. 161, 141.31, &c.

XIX. For similar quibbling on 'Happe' cf. Nos. 23, 36, 190.
25 and . . . softe] Cf. No. 111.24.

XX. There are several of Wyatt's poems, including some in
B, to which this poem may be an answer.

XXII. See Introduction, p. xvi. A rough version of four stanzas
of this poem was printed from Huntington MS. EL. 1160
in Robbins' *Secular Lyrics*:

> I must go walke the woed so wyld,
> & wander here & there
> in dred & dedly ffere;
> ffor where I trusted I am begyld
> & all ffor one.

> Thus am I bannysshed ffrom my blys
> by craft [& false]pretens
> fautles without offens
> and of return no certen ys,
> and all for ffer of on.

> My bed schall be under the grenwood tre,
> a tufft of brakes vnder my hed,
> as on from Ioye were fled;
> thus from my lyff day by do (*day*) I fflee
> and all ffor one.

The Ronnyng stremes shall be my drynke,
    acorns schalbe my foode;
    nothyng may do me good,
but when [of] your bewty I do thynk,
    and all ffor lowe off on.

> Another copy in the same MS, written in the margin, has several variants, the refrain being given in stanzas 1 and 3 as 'and all for your loue my dere'.
> 6 banysshed from my blys] Cf. No. 78.5   66 The Wynter nyghtes that are so cold] Cf. No. 66.27. 74 causers of this stryfe] Cf. Nos. 26.14, 106.21.

XXIII.   Possibly a translation of a renaissance poem, derived ultimately from the Greek Anthology via Ausonius. Cf. Nos. 80, 81, 100.

XXIV.   1 Yf . . . wyll] Cf. No. 51.1.   27 weryd breast] Cf. No. 120.17.

XXVI.   16 clok my wo] Cf. No. 3.14.   37 stedffast ffayth] Cf. No. 130.19.   56 And . . . delayes] Cf. Nos. 139.14, 154.26.

XXVII.   See Introduction, p. xv Written in May 1536, when Mark Smeaton, Lord Rochford, Henry Norris, William Brereton and Francis Weston were executed on a charge of having committed adultery with Queen Anne. Wyatt was imprisoned in the Tower at the same time. See note to XLIII below.   28 in court] if Wyatt wrote the poem, it was presumably after his release.

XXVIII.   10 Cf. No. 154.25.

XXIX.   In MS Add. 18752 the first two stanzas of this poem are followed by the five stanzas of XLV.   11 Rygore] Cf. Nos. 73.6, 134.40, 180.23.   13 deadlye smart] Cf. Nos. 36.8, 74.3, 137.4, 169.8.

XXXIII.   16 knyt the knot] Cf. Nos. 121.26, 125.37, 120.24, 134.7, 169.11, 177.9, 144.34.   19 newffangled] Cf. No. 37.19.   22 Welcomm . . . delight!] Cf. No. 114.35.

XXXIV.   21 ffalshed ffaythe] Cf. Nos. 53.22, 132.23. 23 slaklye tyed may slepe the knot] Cf. Nos. 121.26, 120.24, 134.7, 144.34.   33 swerue] Cf. Nos. 41.12, 134.43, 135.2, 177.18, 182.12.

XXXVI.   1 Spytt off the spytt] Cf. No. 132.22.   4 To be thyn

own assuredlye] Cf. Nos. 109.22, 120.11. 19 swerue]
Cf. note to XXXIV.33 above.

XXXVII. 8 nufanglydnes] Cf. No. 37,19. Wyatt often speaks of
steadfastness and contrasts it with deceit and double-
ness. Cf. Nos. 2.2, 5.15, 5.18, 43.20, 53.34, 69.1,
120.23, 120.25, 143.6. 12 brytell glas] Cf. No.
31.12.

XXXVIII. 10 Cf. Nos. 67.7, 107.21, 129.27, 154.7. 24 wak a
bedde] Cf. No. 137.9 and Chaucer's *Complaint of
Venus*.
27 redresse my smart] Cf. No. 157.5, 10. 28 slept the
knot] See note to XXXIV.23.

XXXIX. Printed by Norman Ault in *Elizabethan Lyrics*. Although
the page is torn, the poem seems complete. 8 my
life to wast] Cf. No. 187.8

XLI. 15 chaunse . . . change] Cf. Nos. 5, 23, 52, 121, 145.

XLII. The third line of each stanza rhymes with the middle
of the fourth. The poem is connected with XLIX.

XLIII. See Introduction, p. xiv for the evidence that this poem
is by Wyatt. It was written during, or soon after,
his imprisonment in the Tower, when he witnessed
the execution of the alleged paramours of Anne
Boleyn. See note to XXVII.
5 *circa Regna tonat*] Seneca, *Phaedra*, 1140. The
imagery of the first two stanzas was suggested by the
same chorus.

XLIV. Perhaps a translation.

XLV. See note to XXIX.

XLVI. In the same hand as XLVII, XLVIII and No. 114.

XLVII. Signed T.W.

XLVIII. Wyatt uses a similar method in No. 71.

XLIX. See note to XLII.

L. 13 kynt the knot] Cf. note to XXXIII.16. 25 prisone
stronge] Cf. II.20 note.

LI. The poem is signed with a monogram, possibly AA.

Appendix A

SOME WYATT POEMS
FROM THE BLAGE MANUSCRIPT

At last withdraw youre crueltye,
  Or let me dy a tons;
Hit ys to mych extremety
  Devysid for the nons,
    To hold me styll alyve   [5
      In paynes styll for to stryve.
    What may I more susteigne?
    Alas! that dy wold fayne,
    And cannot dy for payne.

For to the flame wherwith I burne   [10
  My thought and my desyre,
When into asshes hit shuld turne
  May harte by faruent fyer,
    You send a stormy rayne
      That doth yt quench agayne   [15
    And makes my Eyes expresse
    The teyres doth than redresse
    My lyffe in wretchednes.

Then when they shuld haue drowned
  And ouer whelmed my harte,   [20
The hete doth them confound,
  Renewyng all my smarte;
    Then doth the flame encresse,
    My turment cannot seasse;
    My paynes doth than revyve,   [25
    And I remayne alyve,
    With deth styll for to stryve.

But yf that you wyll haue my deth,
   And that you wold no nother,
Then shortly for to stope my breth   [30
   Withdrawe the one or other;
     For this youre cruelnes
     Doth let yt self doughtles,
    And yt ys reson why
    No man a lyve nor I
    Of dowble deth canne dy.

17 doth than redresse]that dothe opres *later correction.*
32 cruelnes]cruelte *later correction.*   33 doughtles]perde *later correction.*

105   f.170

To wette your yee withoutyn teare,
   And in good helthe to fayne dyssease,
That you therby myn yee myght bleare,
   Therwith your ffrendes to please;
And thoughe ye thynk ye ned not ffeare,   [5
   Yet so ye cannot me apease;
But as you lyst, ffayne, fflatyr or glose,
You shall not wynn yf I do lose.

Prat and paynt and spare not,
   Ye knowe I can me wreke;   [10
And yf so be ye car not,
   Be suer I do not Recke:
And thoughe ye swere yt were not,
   I can bothe swere and speake;
By god and by the crosse,   [15
If I haue the mocke, ye shall haue the worse.

Suffryng in sorrowe in hope to Attayne,
Desyring in ffeare I dar not complayne,
    Trewe in belyefe in whome ys all my trust,
Do thou aplye to ease me of my payne,
    For elys to serue and ssuffer styll I must.   [5

Hope ys my hold, yet in Dyspayre I speake;
I Dryve ffrom tyme to tyme and do not Recke
    How long to love thus after louys lust,
In stody styll of that I dar nor brake:
    Wherffore to serue and suffyr styll I must.   [10

Increas of care I ffynd bothe day and nyght;
I hat that sometyme was my most delyght;
    The cause therof ye know I haue descost,
And yet to Reffrayne yt passythe my myght:
    Wherfor to serue and suffer styll I must.   [15

Love who so lyst, at lenthe he shall well saye:
To love and leve in feare yt ys no playe.
    Record that knoweth, yf this be notyd just,
That wher as love Dothe lede, ther ys no nay,
    But serue and suffer styll allwaye I must.   [20

Then ffor to lyve with losse of lybertye
At last perchaunce shalbe his remedye;
    And ffor his truthe quyted with ffals mistrust,
Who wold not Rew to se whow wrongfullye
    Thus to serue and suffer styll I must.   [25

Vntruthe by trust oft tymes hathe me betrayed,
Mysusyng my hoppe, styll to be Delayed;
    Fortune Allways I haue the fownd vniust;
And so with lyk Reward now hast thou me payed:
    That ys, to serue and suffer styll I must.   [30

7 tyme to tyme]D; tyme B.

114

That tym that myrthe dyd styre my shyppe,
   Whyche now ys fraut wythe euynes,
And fortune bot not than the Lyppe,
   But was defence of my destres,
   Than in my book wrot my mestres: [5
"I am yours, you may be wel suer,
And shall be whyle that Lyffe dothe duer."

But she hyr selffe whyche then wrot that
   Is nou my extryme enemy;
Aboue all men she doth me hat,   [10
   Reioysinge of my mysery;
   But tho that for hyr sake I dy,
I shall be hyrs, she may be suer,
As Longe as my Lyffe dothe induer.

It ys not tyme that can were out,   [15
   Wythe me that whons is fyrmly set;
Whyle nature kypes hyr cours about,
   My hat from hyr no man can Let;
   Tho neuer so soer they me thret,
Yet I am hyrsse, *she may be suer,*
And shallbe whyle that lyff dothe dure.

And onys I trust to se the dey,
   Renuer of my joy and whelthe,
That she these wourdes to me shall sey:
   "In faythe, welcoom" (to me my selffe),   [25
   "Welcoum my hart, welcoum my helthe,
For I am theyn, *thow mayst be sure,*
And shallbe whyle that lyff doth dure".

Ho me alas! What woordes wer thes?
   In coumnant I myt fynd them soo!   [30
I reke not what smart or dysees,
   Tourment or troubel, payne or woo
   I sufferd, so that I myt kno
That she uer myn, I myt be suer,
And should be whyle *that lyff dothe dure.*   [35

20-1, 27-8, 35 *italicised words added from D.*

120   f.173

The knott that furst my hart dyd strayne,
   When that thy servant I becam,
Doth bynd me styll for to remayne
   Always your own, as now I am;
And yff ye fynd that I do fayn,   [5
   Wyth just jugement my self I dam
      To haue dysdayn.

Yf other thowght in me do groo,
   But styll to loue the stedfastly,
Or yff the proffe do nott forth shoo   [10
   That I am yours assuerydly,
Lett euery welth turne me to woo,
   And ye to be contynually
      My chefyst foo.

Yff other thowght or new request   [15
   Do sese my hart, but only thys,
Or yff whythin my weryd brest
   Be hyd on thowght that mene amys,
I do desyer that my unrest
   May styll incres and I to mys   [20
      That I loue best.

Yff in my loue be hyd one spoot
　　Off fals decete and dubbylnes,
Or yff I mynd to slyp the knoot
　　By want of fayth or stedfastnes,　　　　　　　[25
Let all my servys be forgoot,
　　And when I wold haue chefe redres,
　　　　Esteme me nott.

But yff that I consume in payne
　　Wyth burnyng syghes and farvent loue,　　　　[30
And dayly seke non other gayn
　　But wyth my dede thes wordes to proue,
Me thynkes off ryght I shuld obtayne
　　That ye shuld mynd for to remoue
　　　　Your gret dysdayne.　　　　　　　　　　[35

And for a nend off thys my song,
　　In to your handes I do submytt
The dedly grefe, the paynes so strong,
　　Wych in my hart be fyrmly shytt;
And when ye lyst, redres my wrong,　　　　　　[40
　　Sens well ye knoo thys paynfull fytt
　　　　Hath last to long.

9 the]you *later correction.*　　20 incres]hincres MS.　　26 servys]frendshypp
39 in]I B.　　　　　　　　　　　　　　　　　　　　　　　*later correction.*

134

Perdy I sayd hytt nott,
  Nor never thowght to doo,
As well as I ye woott
  I haue no powr thertoo;
And yff I dyd, the lott   [5
  That furst dyd me inchayne
Do never slake the knoott
  But strayter to my payne.

And yff I dyd, ech thyng
  That may do harm or woo   [10
Contynually may wryng
  My hart so hytt goo;
Report may alway ryng
  Off shame on me for aey,
Yf in my hart dyd spryng   [15
  Theys wordes that ye do say.

And yff I dyd ech starr
  That ys in heavyn aboue
May frown on me to mar
  The hope I haue in loue;   [20
And yff I dyd, such war
  As they browght in to Troy
Bryng all my lyfe afar
  From all hys lust and joy.

And yf I dyd so say,   [25
  The bewty that me bound
Incresse from day to day,
  More cruell to my wound,
Wyth all the mone that may
  To playnt may turn my song;   [30
My lyfe may sone decay,
  Wythowt redresse my wrong.

Yf I be clere from thowght,
    Why do ye then complayn?
Then ys thys thyng but sowght   [35
    To put me to more payn.
Then that that ye haue wrowght
    Ye must hyt now redresse;
Off ryght therfore ye ought
    Such rygor to represse.   [40

And as I haue deseruyd,
    So grant me now my hyer;
Ye kno I never swarvyd,
    Ye never fownd me lyer.
For Rakhell haue I seruyd,   [45
    For Lya caryd I never;
And her I haue reseruyd
    Wythin my heart ror euer.

22 they]the MS.   28 wound]D; world B.

1 50   f.66

A! my harte, what alith the
To set soo light be libertye,
Makyng me bound where I was fre?
    A! my harte, A! what ayleth the?

Where thow warte ryde frome all distres,   [5
Voide of all payne and pensyfnes,
To chouse agayne a new mistress,
    A! my harte, A! what ayleth the?

When thow warte well, thow couldes not hold;
To turne agayne thow warte to bolde;   [10
Thus to renew my sorowes olde,
    A! my harte, a! what ayleth the?

Thow knowest full well that but of late
I was turned owt of loues gate,
And now to gyde me to this mate,   [
    A! my harte, a! what ayleth the?

I hopped full well all had ben doone,
But now my hoppe is tane and wone,
To my turment to yeld soo sone,
    A! my hart, a! what ayleth the?

2 be]by   7 chouse]*orig.* chaunge.

151   f.10

Hate whome ye lyste, I care not;
Loue whome ye lyste and spare not;
Doo what ye lyst and fere not;
Sey what ye lyst and dred not;
For as for me, I am not   [
But euyn as on that rekyth not
Whether ye hate or hate not,
For in youre loue I dote not;
Wherfore I pray you forget not,
But loue whome ye lyst and spare not.

1 lyste]*orig.* lyste for.   4 sey]*orig.* make

156   f.120

Love hathe agayne
Put me to payne,
    And yet all ys but lost;
I serue in vayne
And am certayne   [5
    Of all myslyked most.

Both het and cold
Dothe me behold,
    And combres so my mynd
That when I shuld   [10
Speak and be bold
    Yt draweth me styll behynd.

My wyttes be past,
My lyfe dothe wast,
    My comffort ys exyled;   [15
And I in hast
Am lyk to tast
    How love hathe me begylled.

Onles that Ryght
May in her syght   [20
    Optayne pety and grace,
Why shuld a wyght
Haue bewty bryght
    Yf marsye haue no place?

Yet I Alas   [25
Am in suche case
    That bak I cannot goo;
But styll forthe trace
A pacient pace
    And suffer secret woo.   [30

Ffor wythe the wynde
My fyered mynd
   Dothe styll incres in flame,
And she vnkynd   [3
That dyd me bynd
   Dothe torne yt all to game.

Yet can no paygne
Make me reffrayne
   Nor here nor ther to range;
I shall Retayne   [4
Hop to attayne
   A hart that ys so strange.

But I requyer
The paynffull ffyer
   That oft dothe mak me swete   [45
For all my hyer
With lyk desyere
   To geve here hart a hette.

Then shall she prove
How I her love,   [50
   And what I haue her offeryd,
Whiche shuld here move
Ffor to Remove
   The payne that I haue sufferd.

A better ffee   [55
Then she geve me
   She shall of me attayne;
Ffor wher as she
Showyd creweltye
   She shall my hart optayne.

I doo not rejoise not yet complayne;
Both myrth and sadness I do refrayne;
And vse the mene sens folkys wyll fayne;
Yet I am as I am, be hit pleasure or payne.

Men doo juge as they doo trow,   [5
Sum of pleasure, and sum of woo;
Yet for all that nothing they know;
But I am as I am wheresoeuer I goo.

But sens that Judggers take that way,
Let euery man his judgement say;   [10
I wyll hit take in sport and play,
Yet I am as I am whoosoeuer say nay.

Who Judggis well, god well them send;
Whoo Judgith yll, god them amend;
To juge the best therefore intend;   [15
For I am as I am and soo wyll I end.

Yet sum therbe that take delyght
To Judge folkes thowght by outward sight;
But whether they Judge wrong or Right,
I am as I am and soo doo I wright.   [20

I pray ye all that this doo rede,
To trust hit as ye doo your cred,
And thynck not that I wyll change my wede,
For I am as I am how sooeuer I spede.

But how that ys I leue to you;   [25
Judge as ye lyst, false or trew;
Ye know no more then afore ye knew;
But I am as I am whatsoeuer insew.

And frome this mynd I wyll not flye;
But to all them that mysejudge me
I do protest, as ye doo see,   [3
That I am as I am and soo wyll I dy.

5, 8, 19 they]the B.   12 whoosoeuer[woosoeuer MS.

178   f.70

Accusyd thoo I be without desert,
    Noone can hit proue, yet ye beleue hit treue;
Nor neuer yet, sens that ye had my hart,
    Intendid I to be false or untrewe.
Soner I wold of deth susteyne the smart   [5
    Than breke one thyng of that I promast you;
Accept therfore my seruyce in good parte;
    Noon ys a lyve that yll tonges can exstew.
Hold them as false and let not vs depart
    Oure frendship old in hoppe of any new.   [10
Put not thy trust in suche as vse to fayne,
Except thow mynd to put thy frynds to payne

Pas fourthe, my wountyd cries,
  Thos cruel eares to pearce,
Whyche in most hatful wyse
  Dothe styll my playntes reuers.
Doo you, my tears, also [5
  So weet hir bareyn hart,
That pite ther may gro
  And cruelty depart.

For thoughe hard roks amonge
  She semis to haue beyn bred, [10
And wythe tygers ful Longe
  Ben norysshed and fed;
Yet shall that natuer change,
  Yff pyte wons wyn place,
Whome as ounknowne and strange [15
  She nowe auey dothe chase.

And as the water soufte,
  Wytheout forsinge of strength,
Wher that it fallythe oft,
  Hard stonnes dothe perce at Lengthe, [20
So in hyr stony hart
  My playntes at Lengthe shaul grave,
And, rygor set apart,
  Cawse hir graunt that I craue.

Wherfore, my pleyntes, present [25
  Styl so to hyr my sut,
As it, throw hir assent,
  May brynge to me soum frut;
And as she shaul me proue,
  So byd hir me regard, [30
And render Loue for Loue:
  Wyche is my iust reward.

181

Your lokes so often cast,
   Your eyes so frendly rold,
Your syght fyxid so fast,
   All ways one to behold:
Thoughe hyd yt fayne you would,   [
   Yet playnly dothe declaer
Who hathe your hart in hold,
   And wheer goudwil ye baer.

Fayne woulde you fynde a cloke
   Your byrninge fier to hyde,   [10
Yet bothe the flame and smoke
   Brekes out on euery syde:
Ye can not Love so gide
   That yt not issue wynn;
Abrode nydes must it glide   [15
   That burnes so hot within.

For cawse your selff dothe winke,
   Ye iuge all other blynde;
And that Secret you thinke
   That euery man dothe fynde;   [20
In wast oft spend your wynde,
   Your selfe from Loue to quitt,
For agues of that kynde
   Wyl sho who hathe the fytt.

Cawses you fet from far,
   And all to wrap your wo;   [25
Yet ar you neuer the nar;
   Men ar not blyndyd so.
Dyply oft swer you no,
   But all thos othes ar vayne,
So wel your eye dothe sho   [30
   The cawse of all your payne.

Thynke not therfor to hyde
   That styll yt selffe betrays,
Nor syek menes to prouid
   To darke the sonny deys.   [35
Forget thos wontyd weys,
   Leue of dyssemblynge chyer:
Theer woul be found no stays
   To stop a thynge so cleer.

216

To my myshap alas I fynd
   That happy hap ys dangerus;
And fortune workyth but her kynd
   To make the joyfull dolorus.
But all to late hyt cumes in mynd   [5
To wayle the want that made me blynd,
     So often warnyd.

Amydes my myrth and plesantnes
   Such chance ys chansyd sodenly,
That in dyspere to haue redres   [10
   I fynd my chefyst remedy.
No new kynd off vnhappynes
Shuld thus haue left me comfortles,
     So oftyn warnyd.

In better case was never none,   [15
   And yet vnwares thus am I trappt;
My chefe desyer doth cause me mone,
   And to my harm my welth ys hapt:
Ther ys no man but I alone
That hath such cause to syghe and mone,   [20
     So oftyn warnyd.

Who wold haue thowght that my request
    Shuld bryng me forth such bytter frute?
But now ys hapt that I ferd lest,
    And all thys harm cumes by my sute;   [2
For when I thought me happyest,
Evyn then hapt all my chefe vnrest,
      So oftyn warnyd.

Thus am I tawght for to beware,
    And trust no more such plesant chance;   [35
My happy hap hath bred thys care,
    And browght my byrth to grete myschance.
Ther ys no man that hap wyll spare,
But when she lyst hys welth ys bare,
      Thus am I warnyd.

26 thought]D; though B.

218   f.111

I wyll allthow I may not,
    The more yt ys my paygne;
What thow I wyll I shall not,
    Wherffor my wyll ys vayne.

My wyll wylling ys vayne,   [5
    Thus Ryght well ma I see,
Tho wyll wold neuer so ffayne,
    Yet my wyll wyll not be.

Ffor that I wyll and cannot,
    The more I wyll certayne: [10
Thus betwene wyll and shall not
    My wyll I may optayne.

Thus wyshyrs want ther wyll,
    And thay that wyll do crave;
But thay that wyll not wyll   [15
    Ther wyll thay sonest haue.

8 wyll wyll]wyll wyll wyll B.   11 wyll]om. B.

225   f.83

Durese of paynes and grevus smarte
  Hath brought me low and wonderusse weke,
That I cannot cumfort my hart:
  Why syist thou, hart, and wilt not breke?

Thy syghes, thy playntes ar all in vayne;   [5
  The teres voide that from thy yes doo leke;
This lyffe ys dethe, this joye ys payne:
  Why syest thow, hart, and wil not breke?

Thow clymes to catche where ys noo hold,
  Thow stryves where strength ys all to weke,   [10
Thy carefull lyff cannot be told:
  Why syest thow, hart, and wyll not breke?

The faithfuller thow dust endure,
  Les she regarde to here the speke;
And seith pety will not the cure,   [15
  Why syest thow, hart, and wyll not Breke?

As good thow wart asunder ryve,
  As this in thought thy self to breke;
Better were dethe then this alyve
  Euer to sighe and never breke.   [20

Wherefore pety now shuld redresse,
  Orelles come dethe, thy vengeance wreke!
And sens thow fyndes noo gentylnes,
  Harte, syghe no more, I pray the Breke.

6 yes]eyes.   18, 19 this]thus.   21 shuld]*possibly we should read* show.

Appendix B

VARIANTS FROM THE BLAGE MANUSCRIPT

(Readings are those of The Muses' Library edition)

5. 4 soked] stykyd; 6 have I]I haue now; 7 ill] evyll; 9 too] so;
10 sithens] syns; 11 prouf] sorrowe; 24 prevent]present;
26 mele] me; 28 retorne] to torne.

7. 2 helas] alas; 7 leve] must leve; 14 And . . . hold]wyld to be
caught.

16. 4 othres] a nother; 8 gyded] me gyded; 9 full great] gret;
11 very] euery; 13 Then] the; 13 plained] blamyd; 14
reward] reward but.

21. 3 assured . . . I] as sure I haue hit; 5 Ies]yeche; 8 an]a;
9 seketh] seckes; 10 nothing] naught elles; 13 nothing]
naught; 18 hath founde] yet proued; 19 great] but; 20 I do]
doo I; 21 I] that.

34. 1 Madame withouten] Mistris what nedis; 3 And]om.; 5 shall]
may; 6 burneth] bornes; 11 obtain] retayne; 12 myn]my.

39. (The stanzas are given in the following order: 3, 1, 2, 4).
6 they] ye; 10 boeth. . .nyte] that ons I myght; 13 withouten]
of all my; 15 knowe they knowe] wyshe she knoyth; 16
they]she; 16 their] her; 20 For]seth; 21 must be] shalbe.

40. 4 the]om.; 8 you]ye; 9 you standeth]yours standes; 10 Per-
chaunce] may chaunce; 20 Thothre] the tother; 22 taken]
tayne.

51. 4 syns] sith; 10 wepe]syghe; 21 which] and; 29 you] ye;
34 ye] you; 36 none othre] no nother; 37 Therefore]
Wherfore; 38 Restraine] refrayne; 40 And welth away] from
me alway.

66. 9 sigh . . . syng] synge or walle; 11 Rokkes] Rok; 17
thorough] through; 18 By whome, vnkynd] vnkynd al-
thoughe; 21 shall] may; 26 Perchaunce] May chaunce; 30
Care then] but care; 36 Now . . . lute] my lute be styll;
38 is that we] that I have now; 39 Now . . . both]ffor when
this song ys.

68.   1 feet] fayre; 2 fynd] featch; 2 of so wondrous] after so
      strange a

70.   19 verye] wery; 20 regarde yt] regarded.

72.   2 should] shall; 4 relese] redres; 7-14] *om.*; 16 that] yf;
      19 oon slain] me you'v slaine; 24 expresse] exprest; 26
      suche] some; 31-2 And . . . excesse] & exsese of my; 33 you]
      ye; 34 Defamed] disdayned.

78.   1 the] thy; 13 gevest] gevys 22 on] in; 23 any] *om.*

87.   4 no ways that] that no wyse; 5 grownd of] growndyd; 10
      by]at; 12 which doubles]and dubbyl; 13 And] wyth; 14-5
      That . . . refrayne] wych to refrayne/and nott retayne; 27
      That . . . profd] but he hath prouyd; 35 For a short] a small II.
      2 evill] yll; 4 mysuse] abuse; 17 to]*om.* 18 Is but]hytt
      were; 21 chaunce on] changys off; 28 that fully] fully
      that; 29 it] then; 36 men] sum; 38 som] ye; 39 And . . .
      gayne] plesuer for payne III. 2 must] shall; 9 Ye] Yow;
      11 Lest that] and lest; 14 you]ye; 20 the] to; 34 ye] yow;
      38 so]most.

94.   1 From . . . when] As from theys hylles when that; 2 with]
      by; 3 Off . . . that] and of ech thyng; 7 vayleth]ys ther.

Appendix C

POEMS IN THE BLAGE MANUSCRIPT NOT INCLUDED IN THIS EDITION

(I) Wyatt poems also in the Egerton MS. See Appendix B.

(II) Wyatt poems with no substantial variants: Nos. 157, 171.

(III) Surrey poems:
    1. Such wayward wayes hathe loue
    2. Yf Ryght be rakt and ouer Ron
    3. Degrese of Lyghtnes lefte behynde

(IV) Poems by Sir George Blage:
    1. When shall the cruell stormes be past (f.58).
    2. A voyce I haue and yk a will to wayle (f.101).
    3. Let the hethen whiche trust not in the Lorde (f.124).
    4. Ryd of bondage, free from kaer (f.152).
    5. A remembrance of the dethe of the vertuus Lady Quiene Kateryne (f.177).

(V) Poems already published:
    1. Of ffewe wordes sir ye syme to be (Nott, ed. Wyatt, p. 77).
    2. Fortune what aylith thee (*The Court of Venus*).
    3. Some men would think of right to haue (Tottel).
    4. Sustayne, abstayne, kep well in your mind (See p. xiii *ante*).

(VI) Other poems, fragments, doggerel, &c.:
    1. A sobre maide (f.70).
    2. Brome if yow wante yet ought to be loued (f.78).
    3. Cursyd be he that first began (f.82).
    4. Danger thy selff led for nothyng (f.91).
    5. From Adams fall to Noes noyfull floud (f.92).
    6. O Ioue geve eare vnto my cry (f.94).
    7. Where shall my lyeue (f.111).
    8. In sommer seson as soune as the Sonne (f.115).
    9. Love who so wyll whyt bread I best do love browne (f.121).
    10. Alas your ffondnes makys me smylle (f.121).

11. My lady ys suche one to whom our Lord hath lent (f.127).
12. O lord what chance what thyng ys thys (f.136).
13. O faythfull hart plungyd in distress (f.140).
14. Only the Elect on the Sabbath doth praye (f.153).
15. Bragg not of goodes (f.153).
16. Repentance ramsom of each offence (f.174).
17. When many dayes and nyghtes in grefe were paste (f.180).